RECORDED VERSIONS GUITAR

AUTHENTIC TRANSCRIPTIONS
WITH NOTES AND TABLATURE

THE VERY BEST OF
PAUL WESTERBERG
& THE REPLACEMENTS

T0066618

2	ALEX CHILTON	73	I'LL BE YOU
13	AS FAR AS I KNOW	90	JOHNNY'S GONNA DIE
19	BASTARDS OF YOUNG	104	LET THE BAD TIMES ROLL
30	CAN'T HARDLY WAIT	117	MERRY GO ROUND
37	COLOR ME IMPRESSED	131	SHIFTLESS WHEN IDLE
43	DYSLEXIC HEART	141	SKYWAY
60	HERE COMES A REGULAR	147	UNSATISFIED
64	I WILL DARE		

Music transcriptions by Aurélien Budynek, Scott Kulman, Kevin Langan, and Martin Shellard

Cover photo: Marc Norberg

ISBN 978-1-4234-9291-7

HAL•LEONARD® CORPORATION
7777 W. BLUEMOUND RD. P.O. BOX 13819 MILWAUKEE, WI 53213

In Australia Contact:
Hal Leonard Australia Pty. Ltd.
4 Lentara Court
Cheltenham, Victoria, 3192 Australia
Email: ausadmin@halleonard.com.au

Visit Hal Leonard Online at
www.halleonard.com

from *Pleased to Meet Me*

Alex Chilton

Words and Music by Paul Westerberg, Tommy Stinson and Christopher Mars

Gtrs. 1 & 4: Open A tuning:
(low to high) E-A-E-A-C#-E

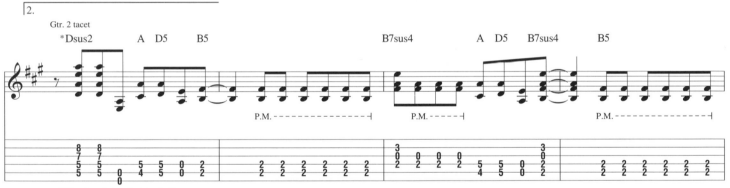

*Chord symbols reflect implied harmony.

Pre-Chorus

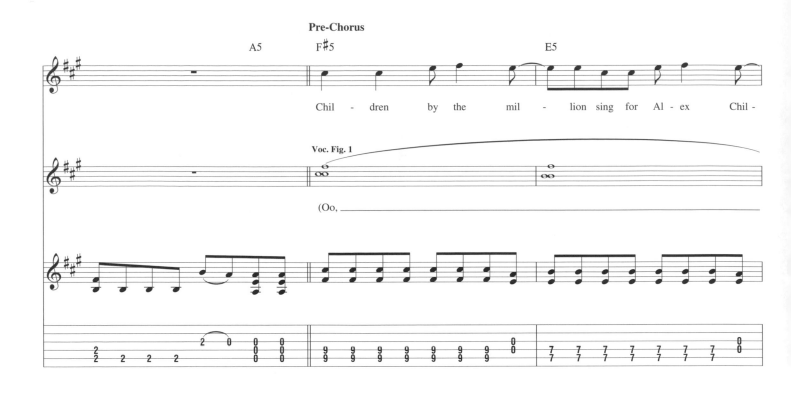

Chil - dren by the mil - lion sing for Al - ex Chil -

(Oo, _____

Chorus

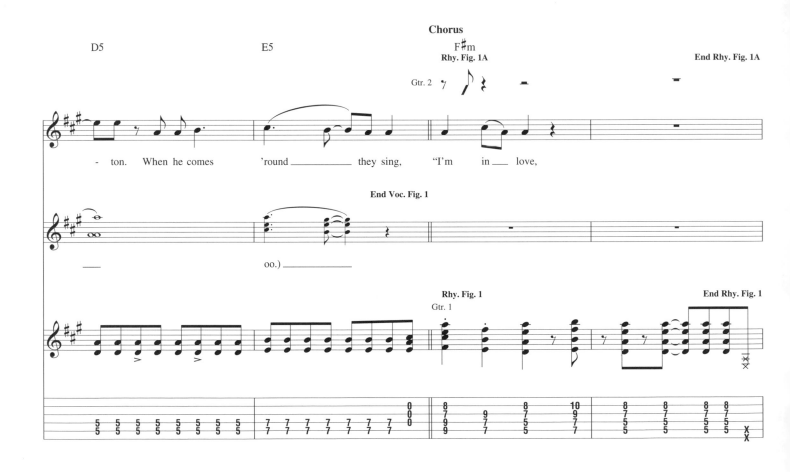

\- ton. When he comes 'round _____ they sing, "I'm in ___ love,

__ oo.) _____

Gtrs. 1 & 2: w/ Rhy. Figs. 1 & 1A (2 1/2 times)

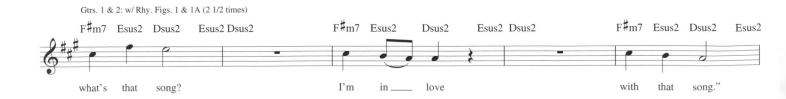

what's that song? I'm in ___ love with that song."

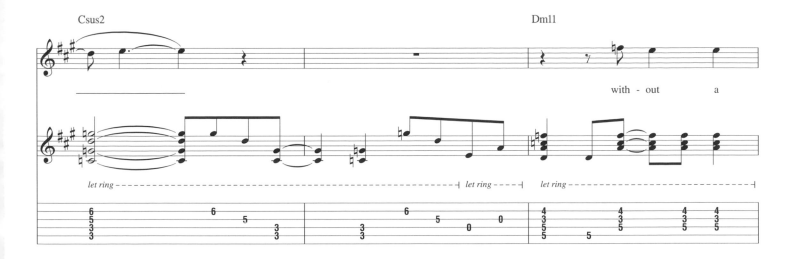

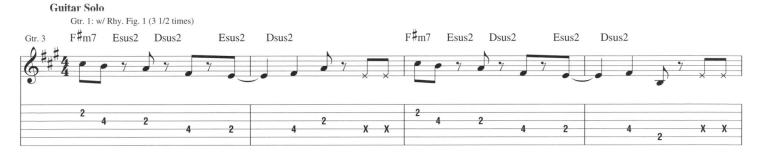

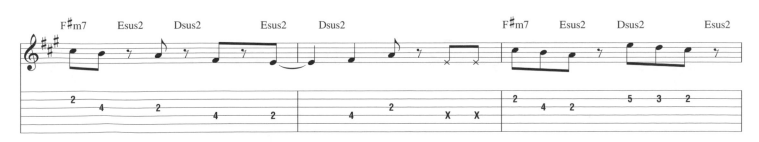

Pre-Chorus

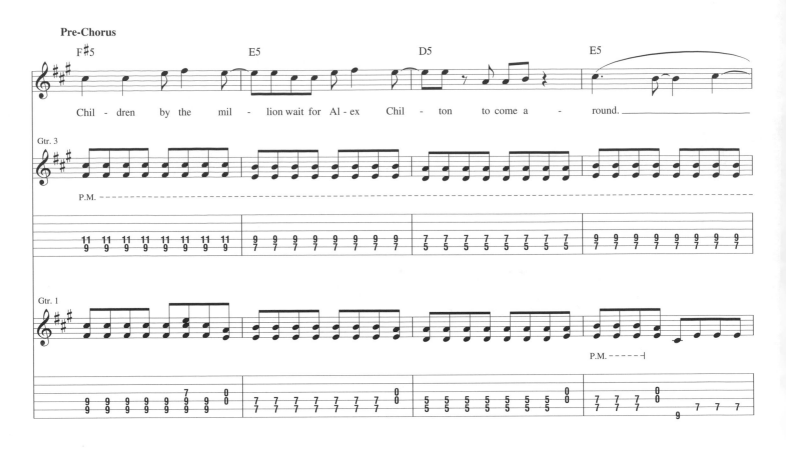

Chil-dren by the mil-lion wait for Al-ex Chil-ton to come a - round.

Chorus

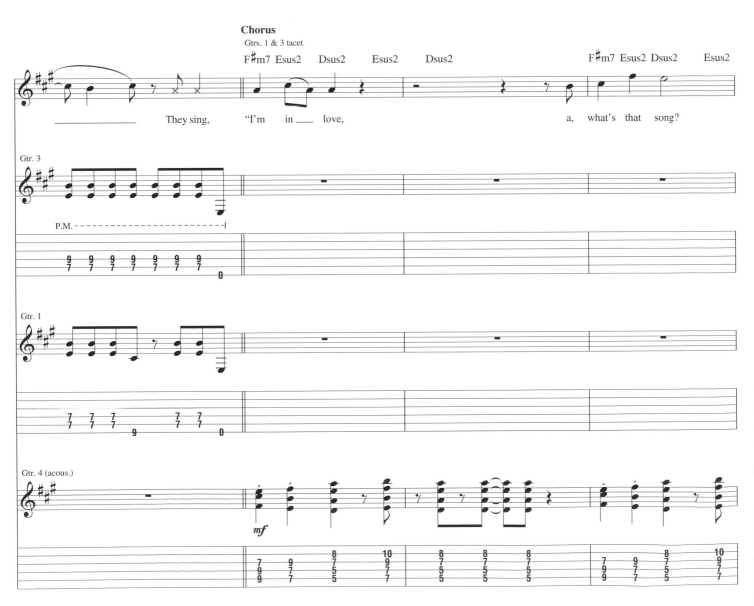

They sing, "I'm in love, a, what's that song?

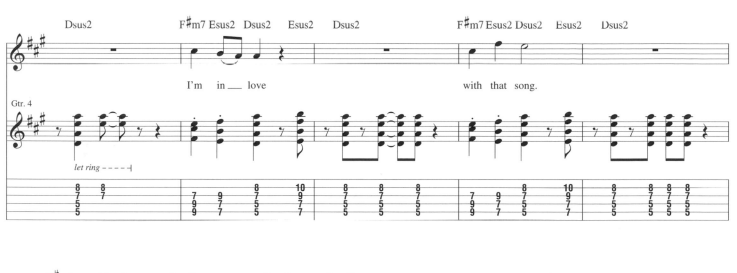

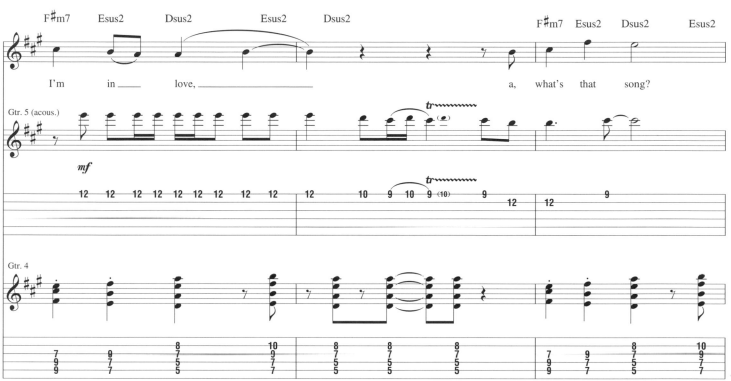

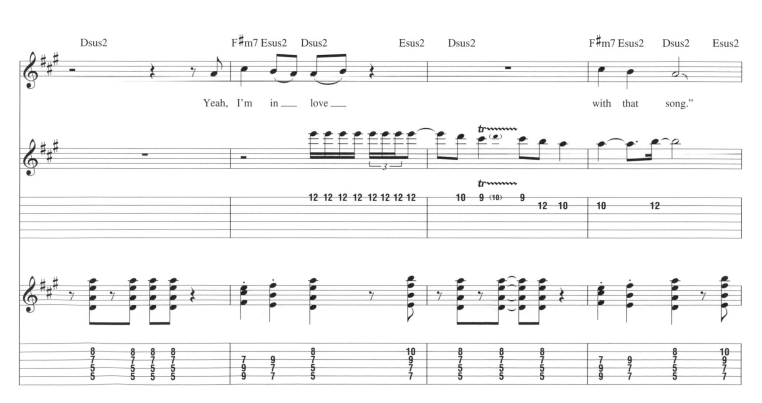

12

from *Folker*

As Far As I Know

Words and Music by Paul Westerberg

Gtrs. 1 & 2: Open A tuning, down 1/2 step:
(low to high) E♭-A♭-C-E♭-A♭-C

Gtrs. 3 & 4: Tune down 1/2 step:
(low to high) E♭-A♭-D♭-G♭-B♭-E♭

Intro

Moderately ♩ = 134

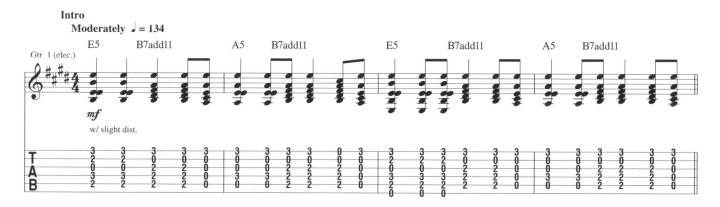

Verse

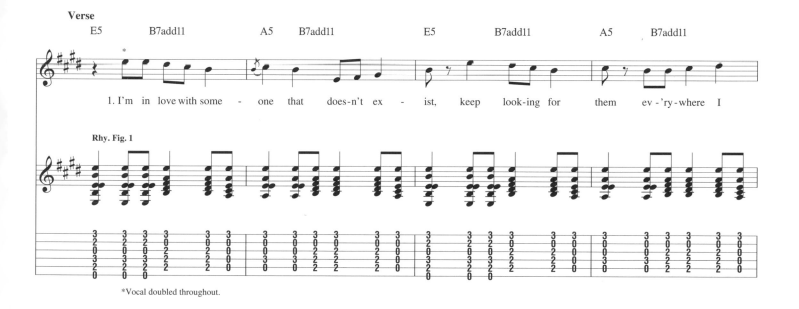

1. I'm in love with some - one that does-n't ex - ist, keep look-ing for them ev-'ry-where I

Rhy. Fig. 1

*Vocal doubled throughout.

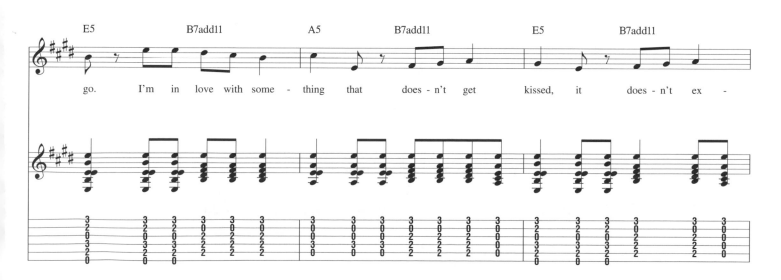

go. I'm in love with some - thing that does - n't get kissed, it does - n't ex -

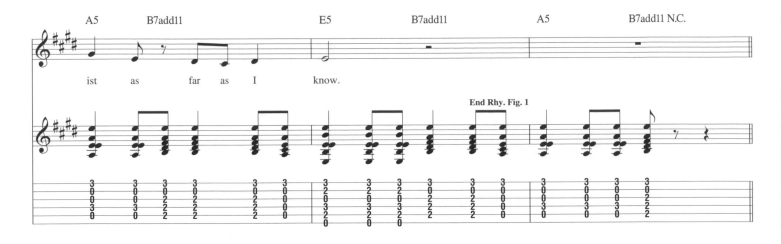

A5   B7add11   E5   B7add11   A5   B7add11 N.C.

ist as far as I know.

End Rhy. Fig. 1

Verse

*Gtrs. 1 & 2: w/ Rhy. Fig. 1

E5   B7add11   A5   B7add11   E5   B7add11

2. I'm in love with a face that I've nev - er seen once up - on a

*Gtr. 2 (elec.) w/ slight dist., played *mf*.

A5   B7add11   E5   B7add11   A5   B7add11

place long time a - go. I'm in love with a time that nev - er took

Gtrs. 1 & 2: w/ Rhy. Fill 1

E5   B7add11   A5   B7add11   E5   B7add11   A5   B7add11

place, that's eas - y to trace as far as I know.

𝄋 Chorus

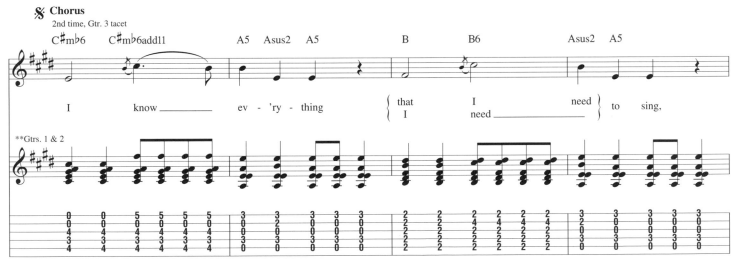

2nd time, Gtr. 3 tacet

C#m♭6 C#m♭6add11 A5 Asus2 A5   B B6   Asus2 A5

I know ev - 'ry - thing { that I need } to sing,
                            { I need }

**Gtrs. 1 & 2

**Composite arrangement

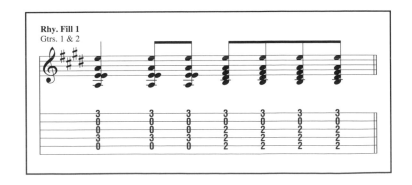

Rhy. Fill 1
Gtrs. 1 & 2

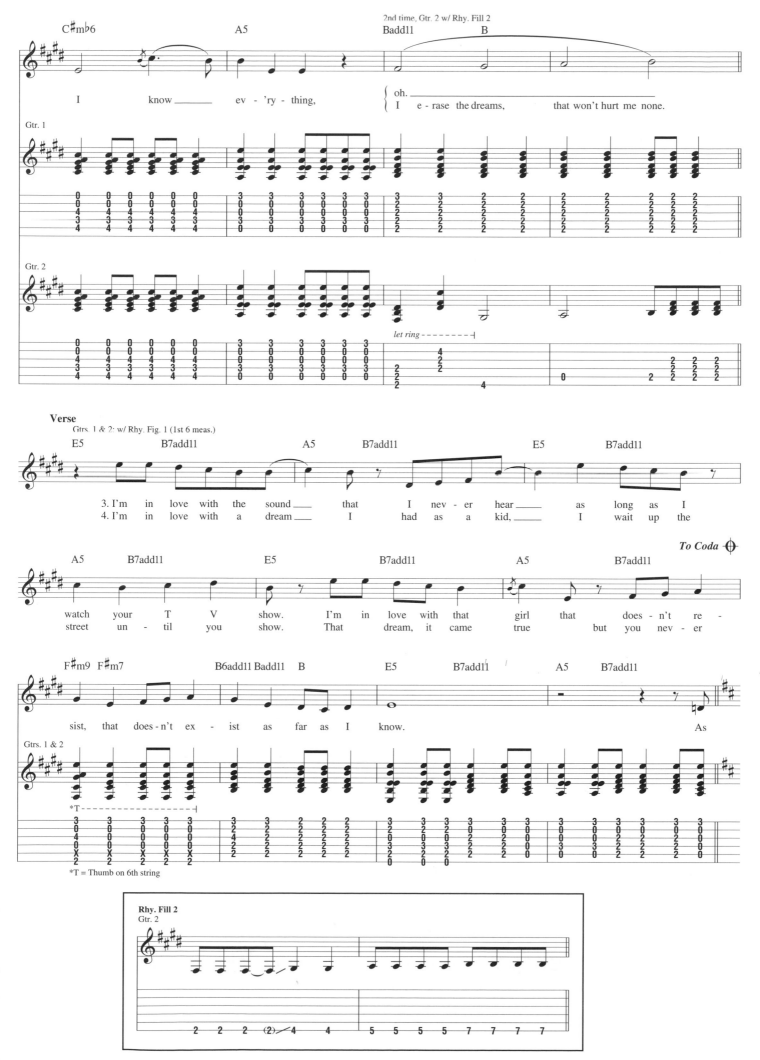

Bridge

far as I ___ know,   stars in the sky are   dull. ___   As

far as I know,   com - pared to your eyes, ___   oh. ___

As

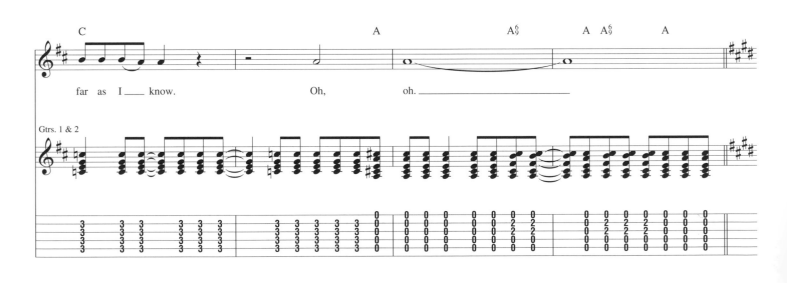

far as I ___ know.   Oh,   oh. ___

Interlude

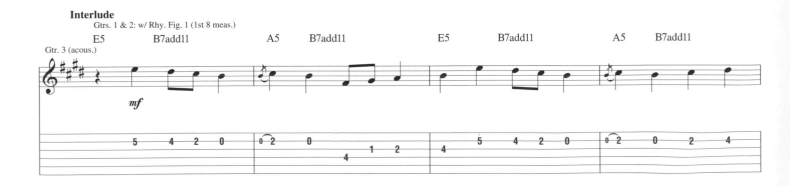

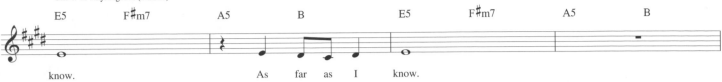

know.   As   far   as   I   know.

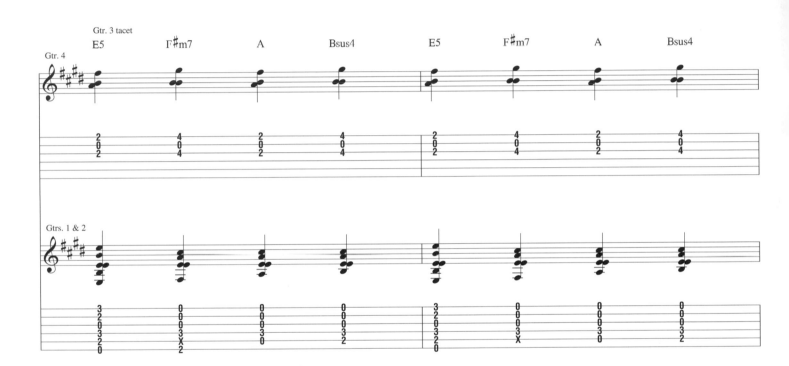

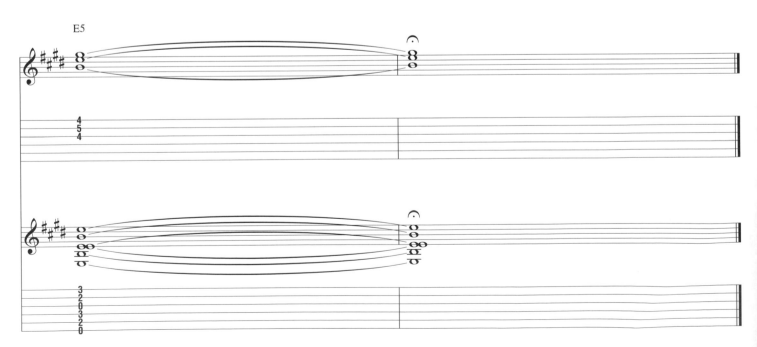

from *Tim*

Bastards of Young

Words and Music by Paul Westerberg

*Chord symbols reflect basic harmony.

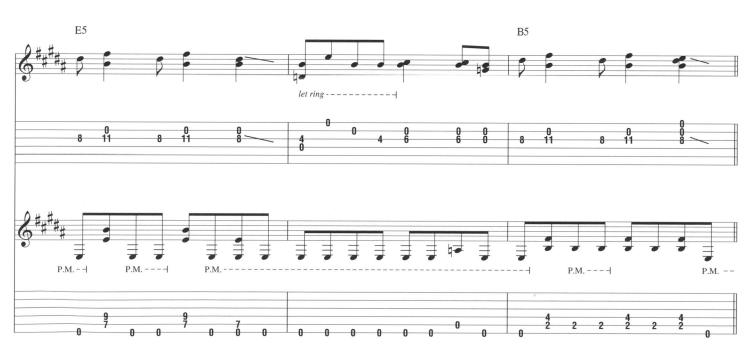

Verse

Guitar Solo

3. The

⊕ Coda

Chorus

We are the sons of no one, bas-tards of young.

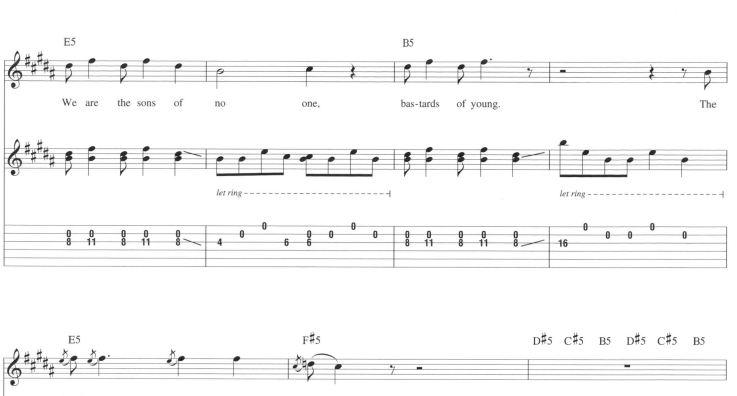

We are the sons of no one, bas-tards of young. The

daugh-ters and the sons. ___

Young. ___

Young.

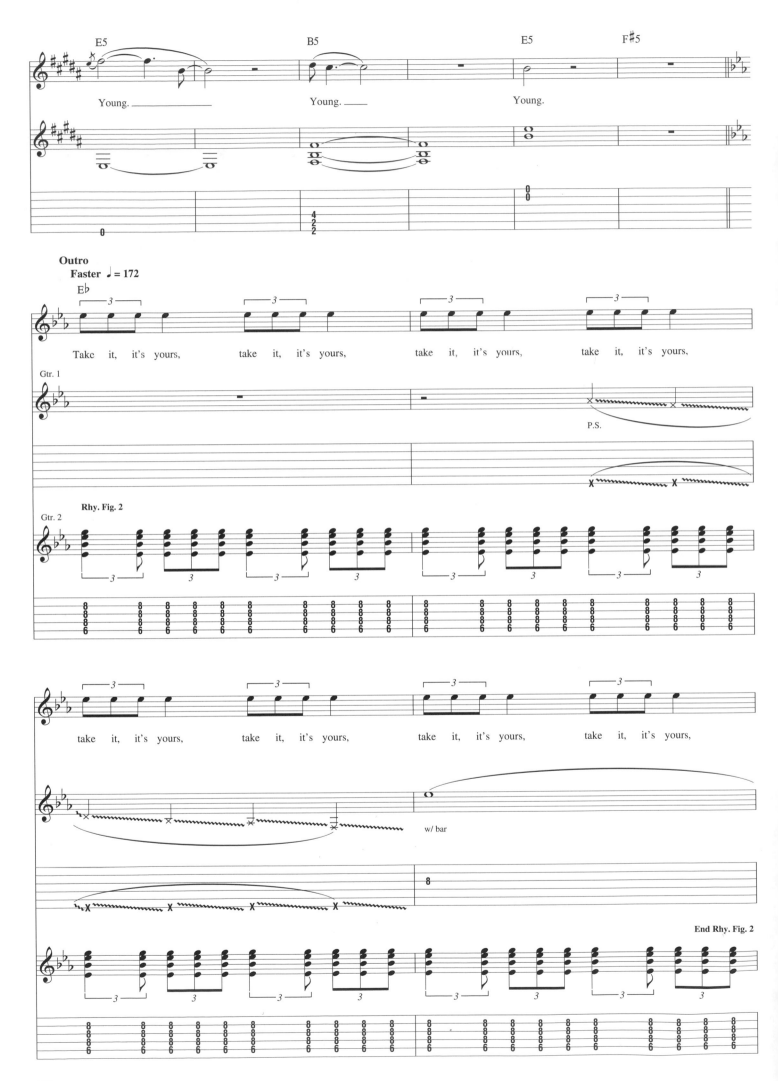

take it, it's yours.

from *Pleased to Meet Me*

Can't Hardly Wait

Words and Music by Paul Westerberg

Intro
Moderately fast ♩ = 140

N.C.

Gtr. 3 (acous.)

mf

(cont. in notation)

1. I'll

Riff A
Gtr. 1 (elec.)

End Riff A

mf
w/ clean tone

Riff A1
Gtr. 2 (elec.)

End Riff A1

mf
w/ clean tone

Verse
Gtrs. 1 & 2: w/ Riffs A & A1 (4 times)

D   G

write   you ___ a   let-ter   to-mor-row,   to-

Rhy. Fig. 1
Gtr. 3

End Rhy. Fig. 1

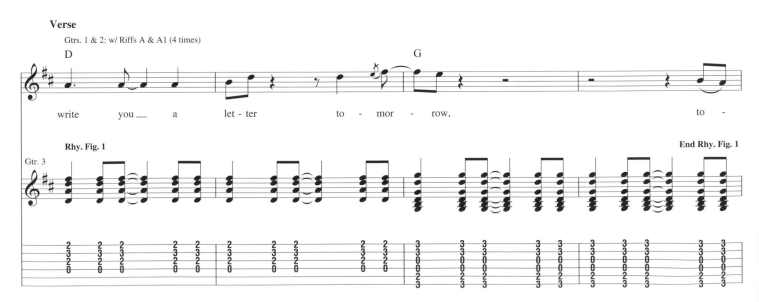

Verse

Gtrs. 1 & 2: w/ Riffs A & A1 (2 times)
Gtr. 3: w/ Rhy. Fig. 1 (2 times)

2. Je - sus rides be - side ___ me. He

nev - er buys __ an - y ___ smokes. __

Hur - ry up, hur - ry up, ain't _ you had e - nough of this stuff?

Ash - tray floors, dirt - y clothes and filth - y jokes. ___

Bridge

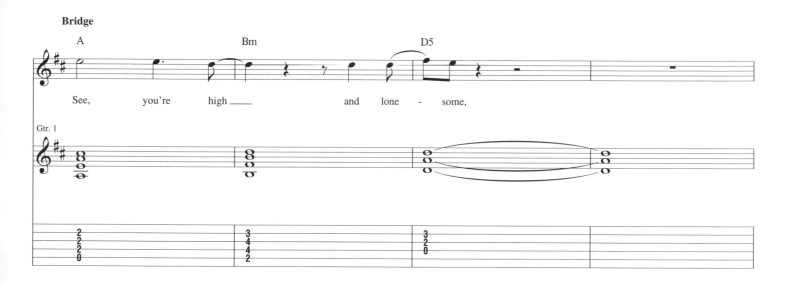

See, you're high ___ and lone - some,

Gtr. 1

try and try ___ and try. ___

Interlude

Chorus

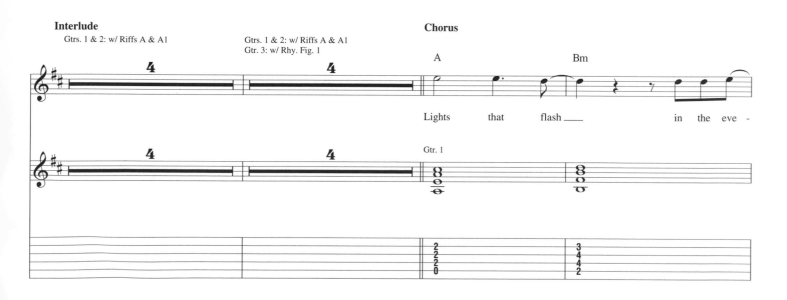

Lights that flash ___ in the eve -

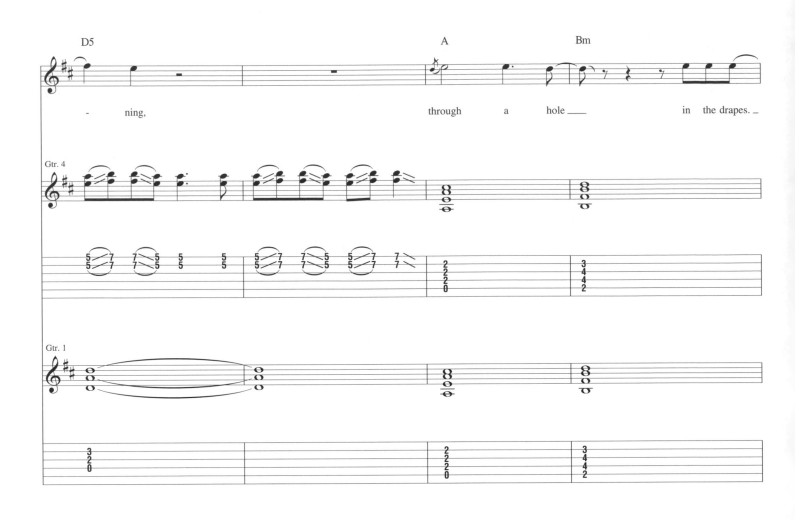

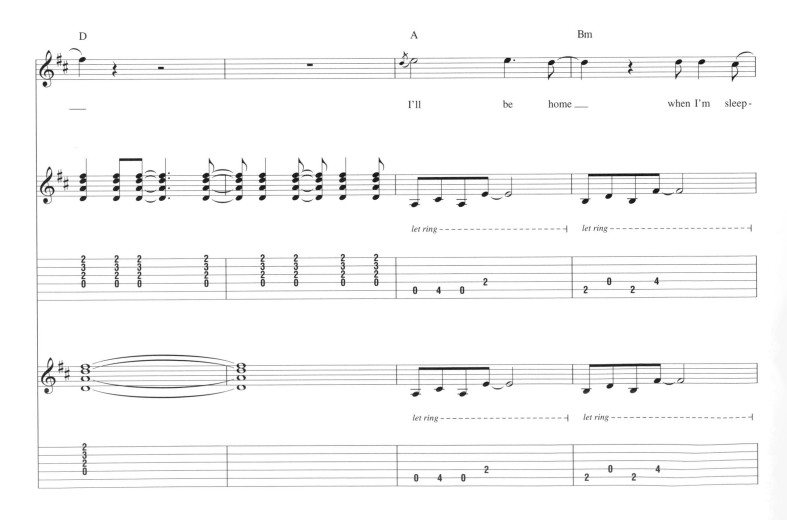

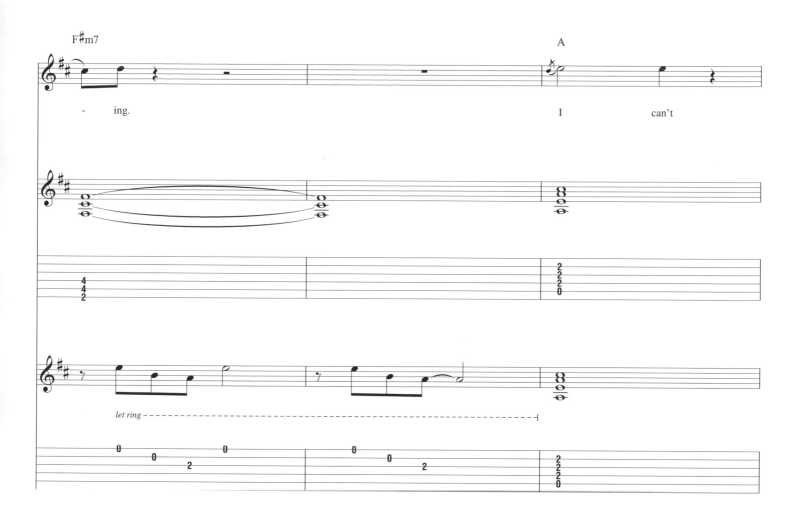

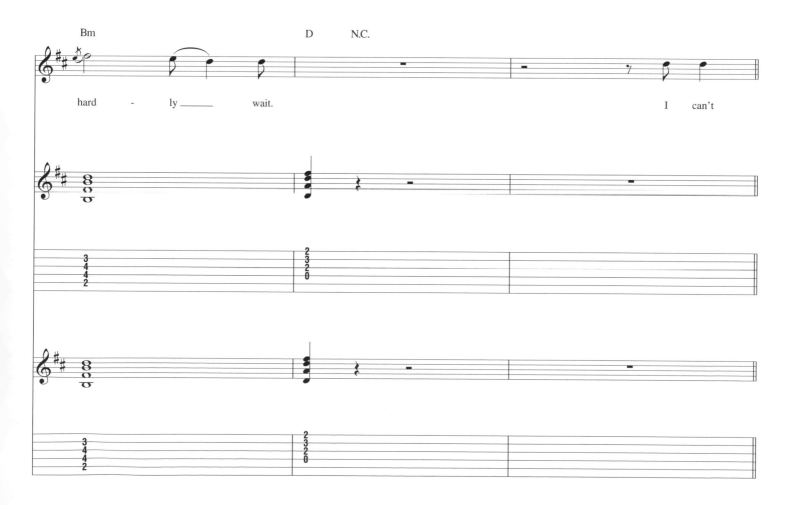

Outro

Gtrs. 1 & 2: w/ Riffs A & A1 (last 2 meas.)
Gtr. 3: w/ Rhy. Fig. 1 (last 2 meas.)
Gtr. 4 tacet

Gtrs. 1 & 2: w/ Riffs A & A1 (till fade)
Gtr. 3: w/ Rhy. Fig. 1 (till fade)

Color Me Impressed

Words and Music by Paul Westerberg

Verse

Gtr. 1: w/ Rhy. Fig. 1 (2 times)
Gtr. 2 tacet

mon - key on ____ the mir - ror, oh shit, pass ____ the bill to Chris,

in - tox - i - cat - ed lov - er end - ing our ____ French kiss. ____

Can you stand me on my ___ feet? ___

Gtr. 1

Can you stand me on my

D.S. al Coda

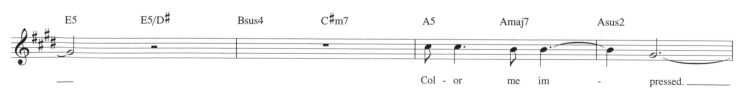

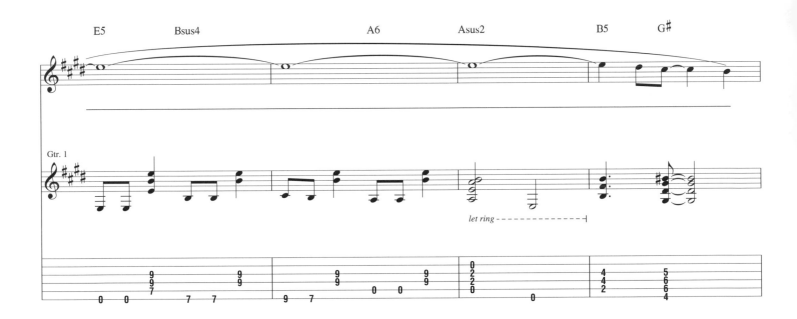

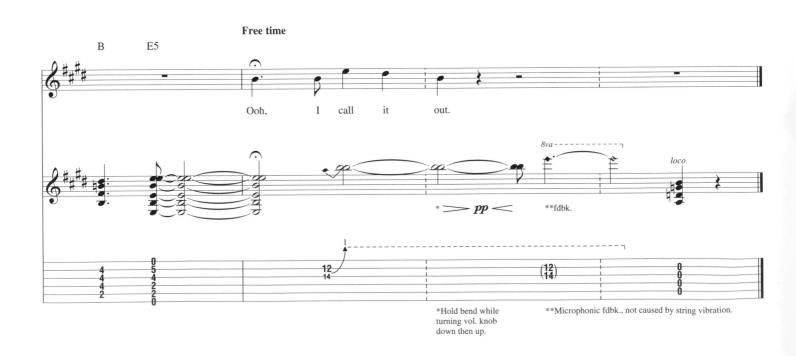

Dyslexic Heart

Words and Music by Paul Westerberg

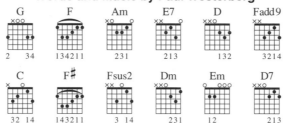

Intro
Moderately ♩ = 136

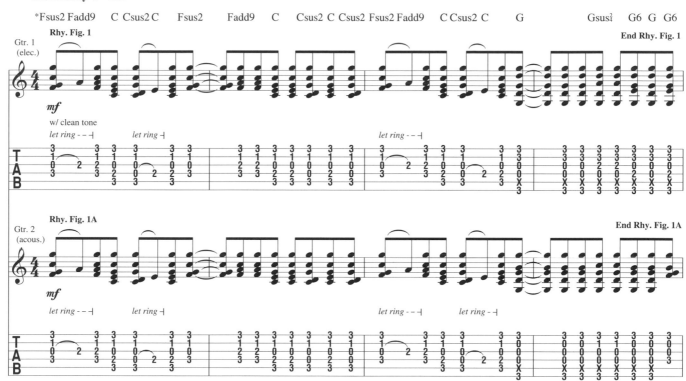

*Chord symbols reflect overall harmony.

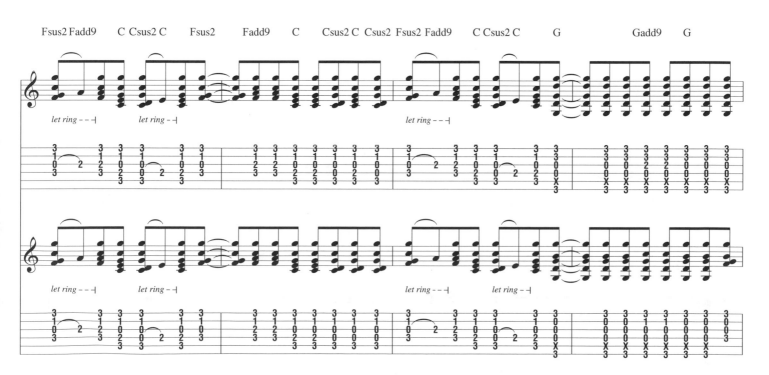

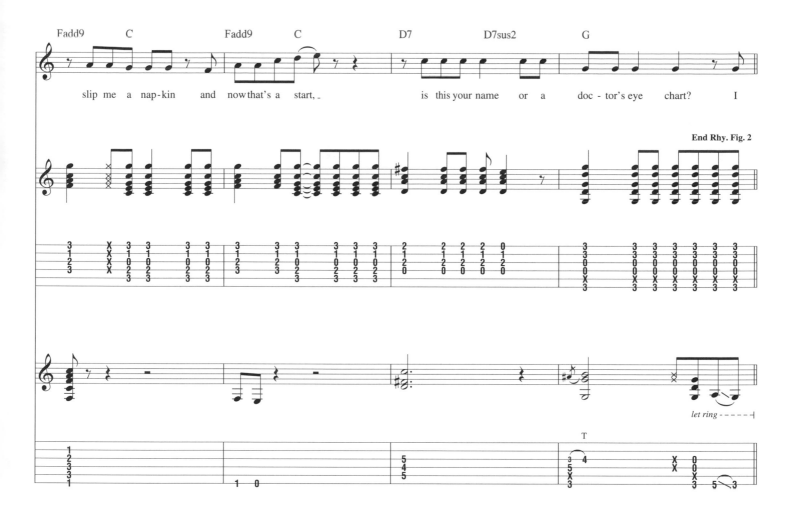

slip me a nap-kin and now that's a start, ___ is this your name or a doc-tor's eye chart? I

Chorus

try and com-pre-hend you but I got a dys-lex-ic heart. ___

I ain't dy-ing to of-fend you, I got a dys-lex-ic heart.

Oh, oh, oh.

End Rhy. Fig. 3

let ring

let ring

let ring

let ring

Verse

Gtrs. 1 & 2: w/ Rhy. Fig. 2

2. Thanks for the book, now my ta-ble is read-y, a li-brar-y or a bar?

Gtr. 3

Be-tween the cov-ers I judged you were read-y, a half an-gel, half tart. Ooh, I

Chorus

Gtrs. 1 & 2: w/ Rhy. Fig. 3

try and com-pre-hend you but I got a dys-lex-ic heart. __ Oh! I ain't

dy - in' to of -fend you, I got a dis - lex - ic heart. ___

Do I read you cor-rect - ly, you need me di - rect - ly?

Gtr. 4

Gtrs. 1 & 2

let ring

Gtr. 3

let ring

say - in'?   Think - in' 'bout stay - in'?   Are you just play -

- ing, __ mak-ing pass - es,   well, my heart __ could use __ some glass - es. _____

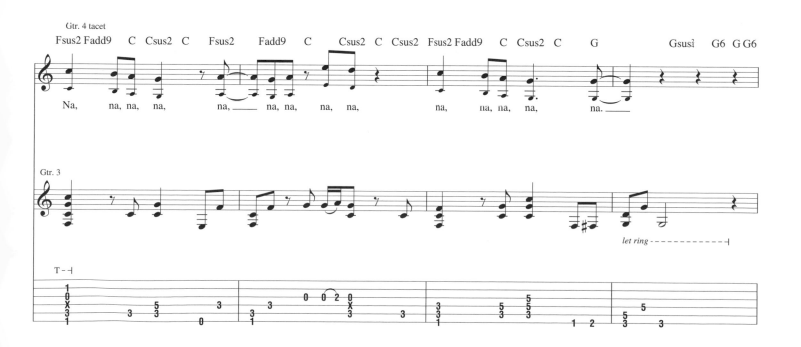

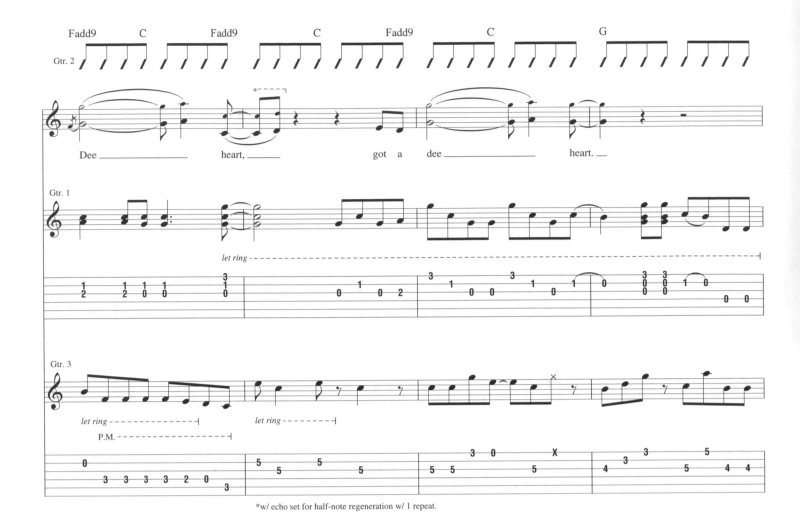

*w/ echo set for half-note regeneration w/ 1 repeat.

**As before

Mm.

Interlude

Gtr. 4 tacet

Dee _____ heart, _____ a dee _____ heart, _____ a

*w/ echo set for half-note regeneration w/ 1 repeat.

*w/ echo set for half-note regeneration w/ 1 repeat.

Outro

Voc.: w/ Voc. Fig. 1 (till fade)
Gtrs. 1 & 2: w/ Rhy. Fig. 4 (till fade)

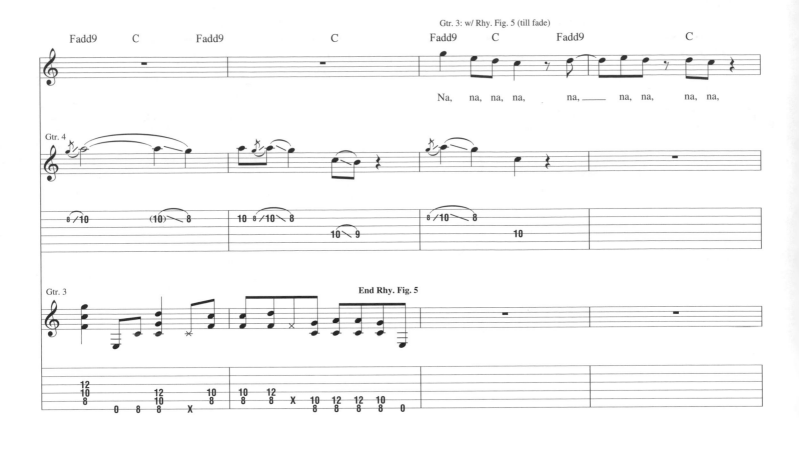

na, na, na, na, na, na, na, na, na. Na, na, na, na, na, na, na, na, na,

na, na, na, na, na, na, na, na. Na, na, na, na, na,

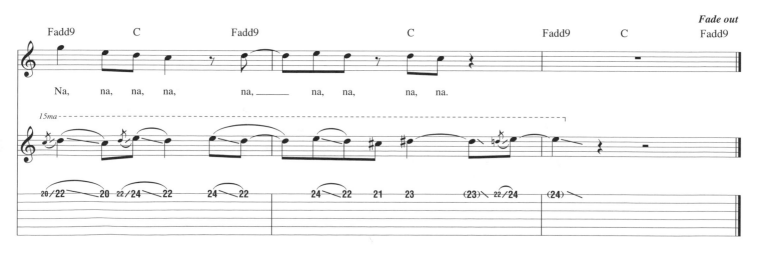

na, na, na, na, na, na, na, na, na.

Na, na, na, na, na, na, na, na, na.

from *Tim*

Here Comes a Regular

Words and Music by Paul Westerberg

Capo VI

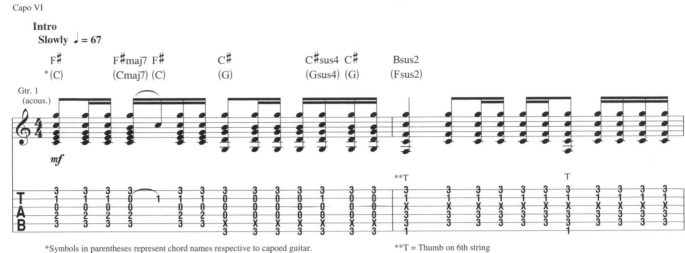

*Symbols in parentheses represent chord names respective to capoed guitar.
Symbols above reflect actual sounding chords. Capoed fret is "0" in tab.

**T = Thumb on 6th string

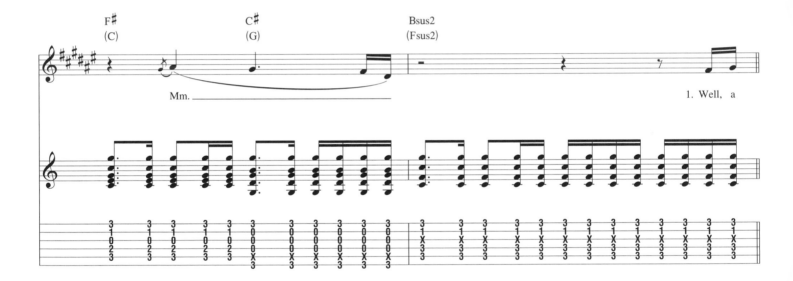

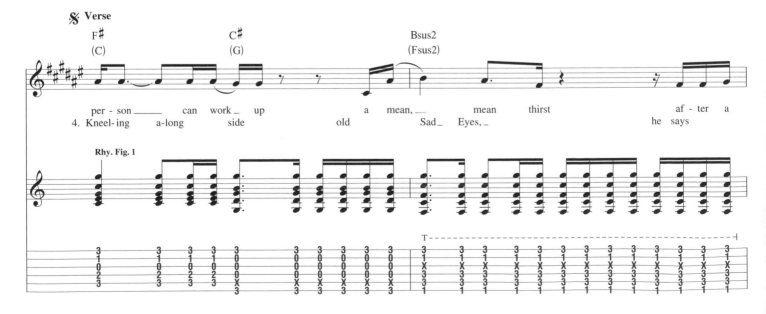

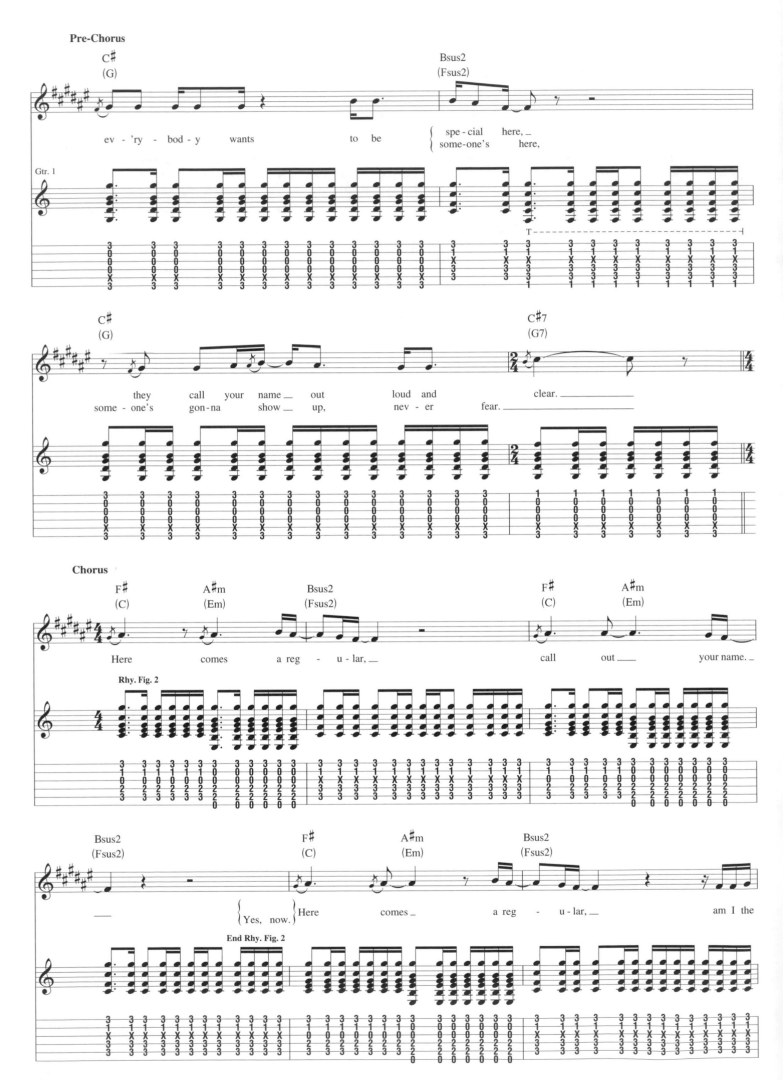

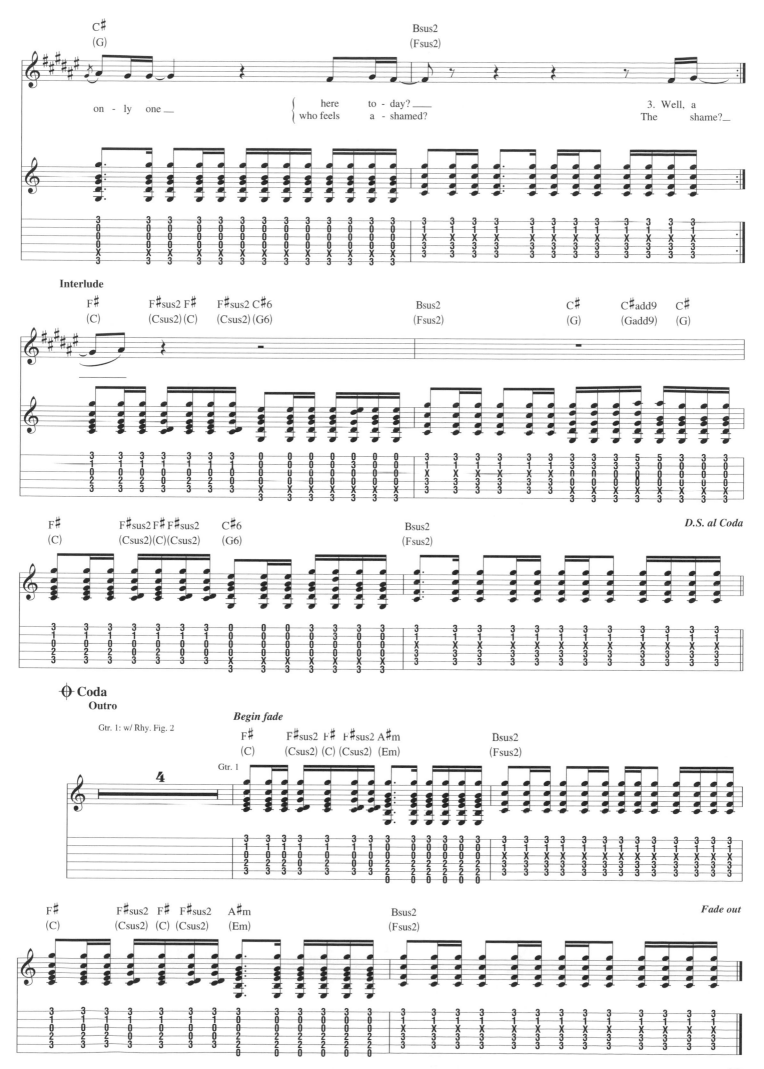

from *Let It Be*

I Will Dare

Words and Music by Paul Westerberg

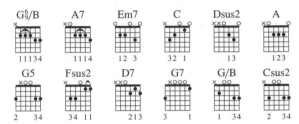

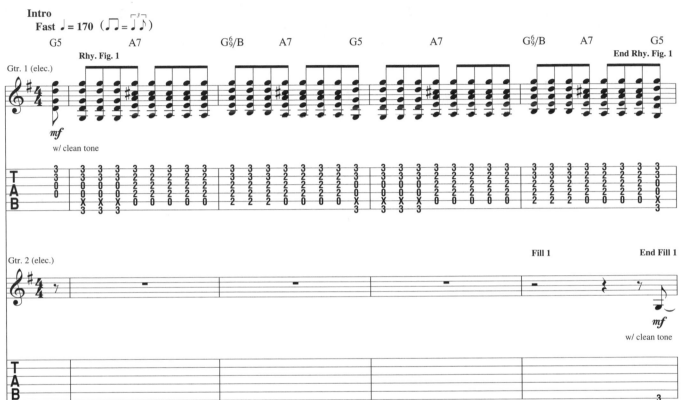

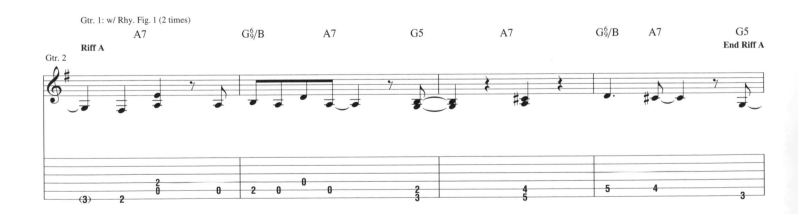

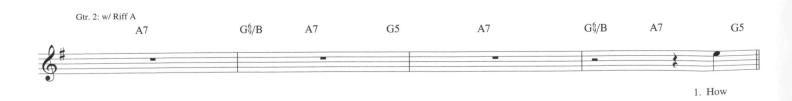

Verse

Gtr. 1: w/ Rhy. Fig. 1 (2 times)
Gtr. 2: w/ Riff A (2 times)

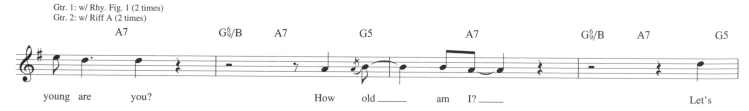

young are you? How old ___ am I? ___ Let's

count the rings ___ a - round __ my __ eyes. ___

Interlude

Gtr. 1: w/ Rhy. Fig. 1
Gtr. 2: w/ Riff A

Verse

Gtr. 1: w/ Rhy. Fig. 1 (1 3/4 times)
Gtr. 2: w/ Riff A (1 3/4 times)

2. How _ smart are you? How dumb am I?

Don't count an - y of my ad - vice. __

Chorus

Oh, meet me an-y-place, or an-y-where, or an-y-time, __ now I don't

Hey!

Play, play.

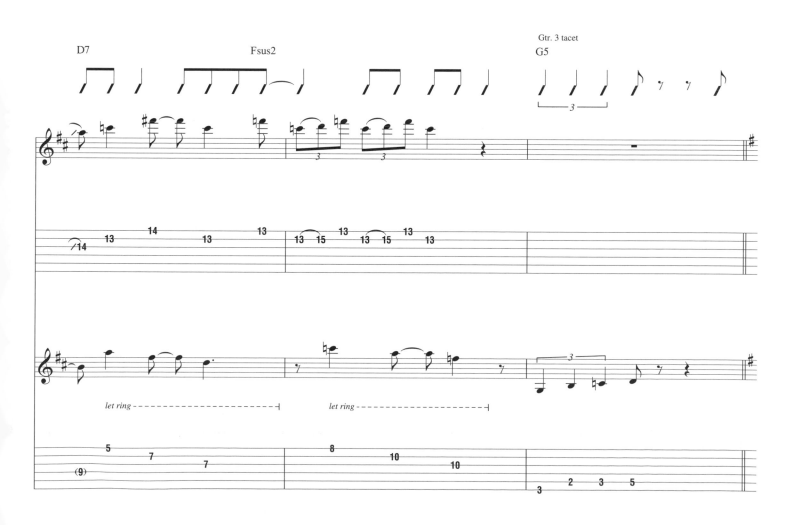

from *Don't Tell a Soul*

I'll Be You

Words and Music by Paul Westerberg

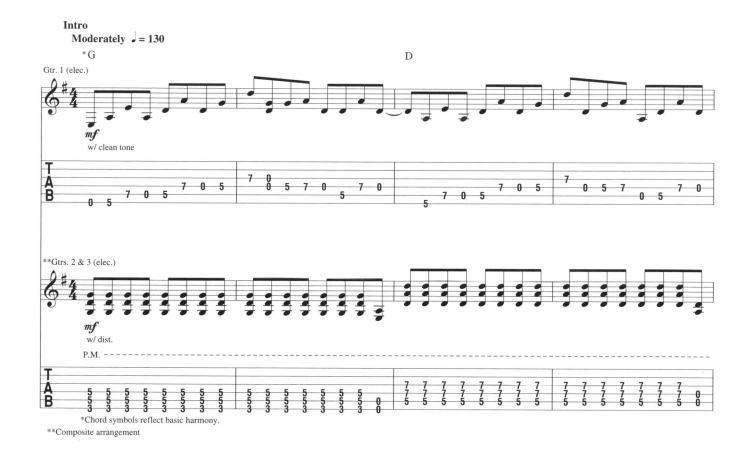

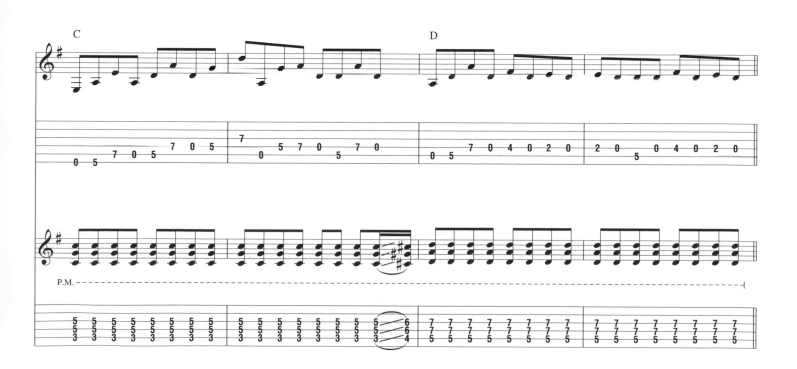

*Chord symbols reflect basic harmony.

**Composite arrangement

Verse

Gtr. 1 tacet

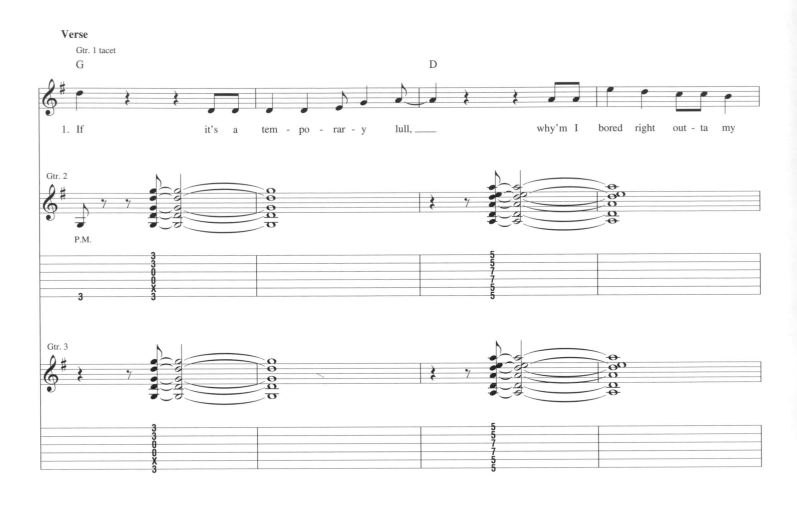

1. If it's a tem-po-rar-y lull, _____ why'm I bored right out-ta my

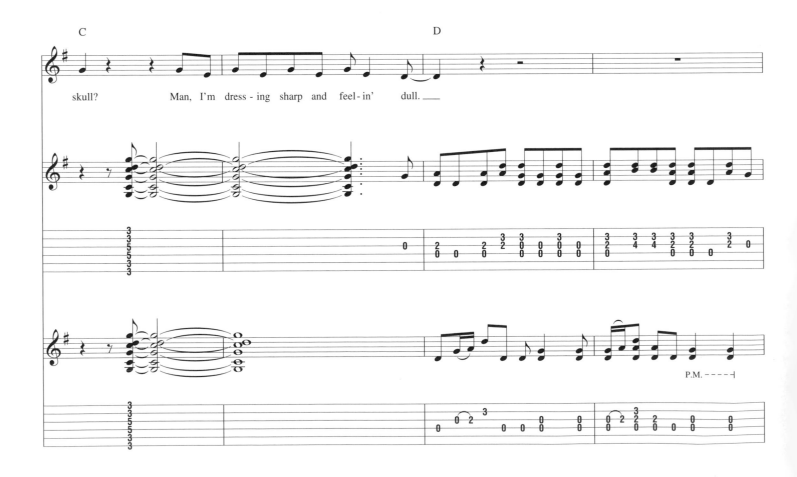

skull? Man, I'm dress-ing sharp and feel-in' dull. _____

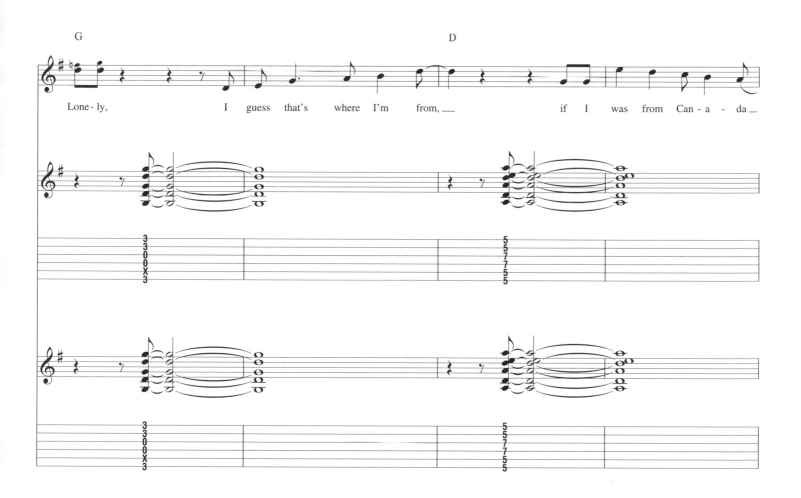

Lone-ly, I guess that's where I'm from, ___ if I was from Can-a-da ___

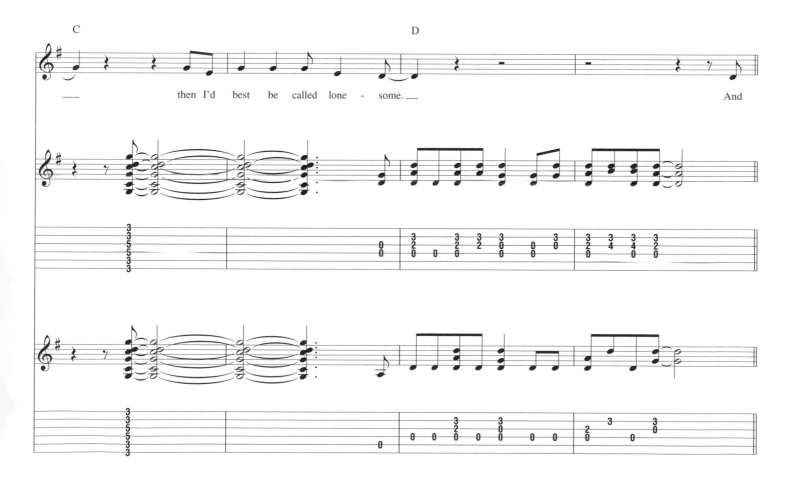

___ then I'd best be called lone-some. ___ And

Chorus

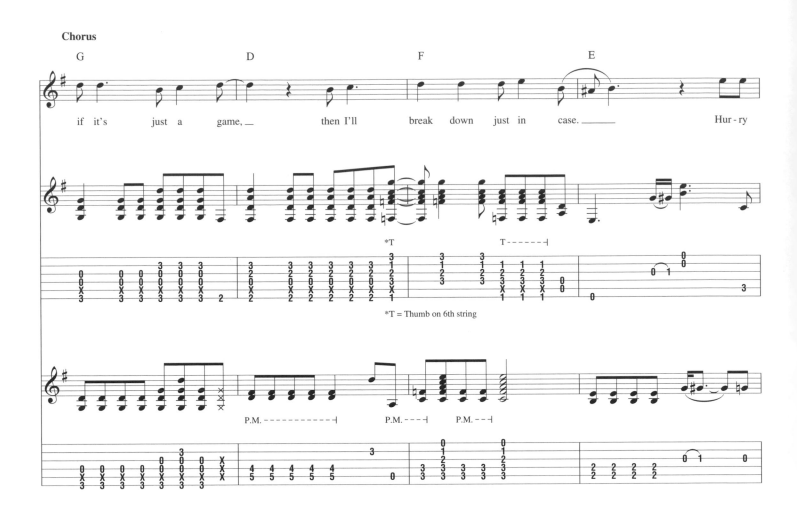

if it's just a game,— then I'll break down just in case. _____ Hur - ry

*T = Thumb on 6th string

up,
(Hur - ry up.)
we're run - nin' in our ___ last race. ___
2. Well, I

Chorus

purge my soul per - haps, ___ for the im - mi - nent ___ col - lapse. ___ Oh,

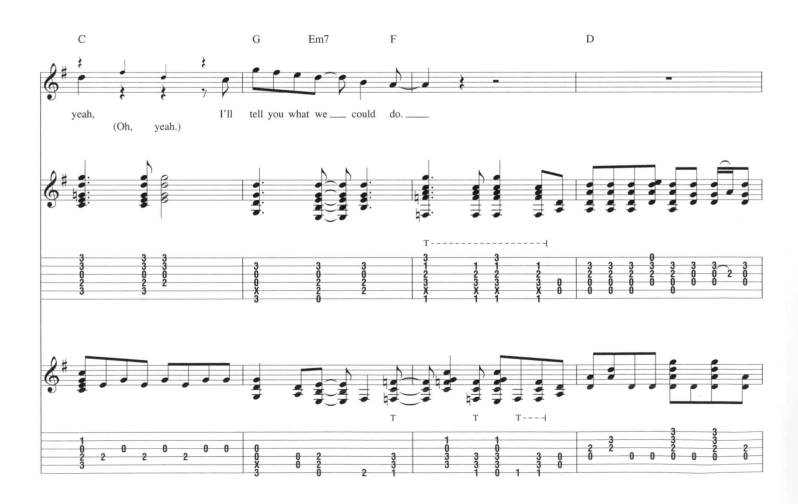

yeah, I'll tell you what we ___ could do. ___ Oh,
(Oh, yeah.)

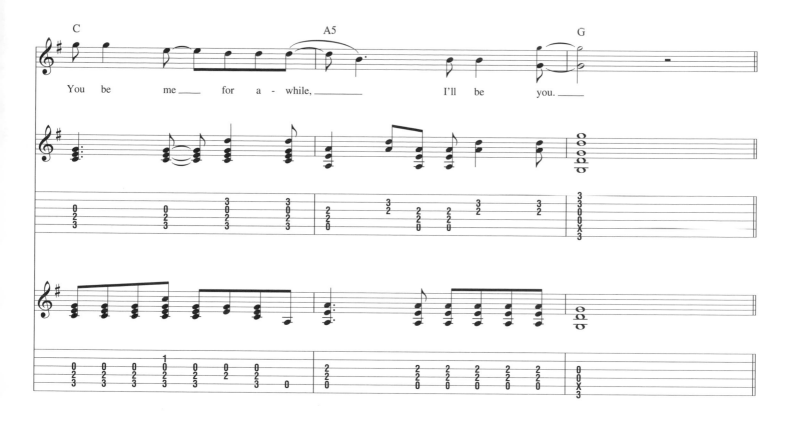

You be me ___ for a - while, ___ I'll be you. ___

Guitar Solo

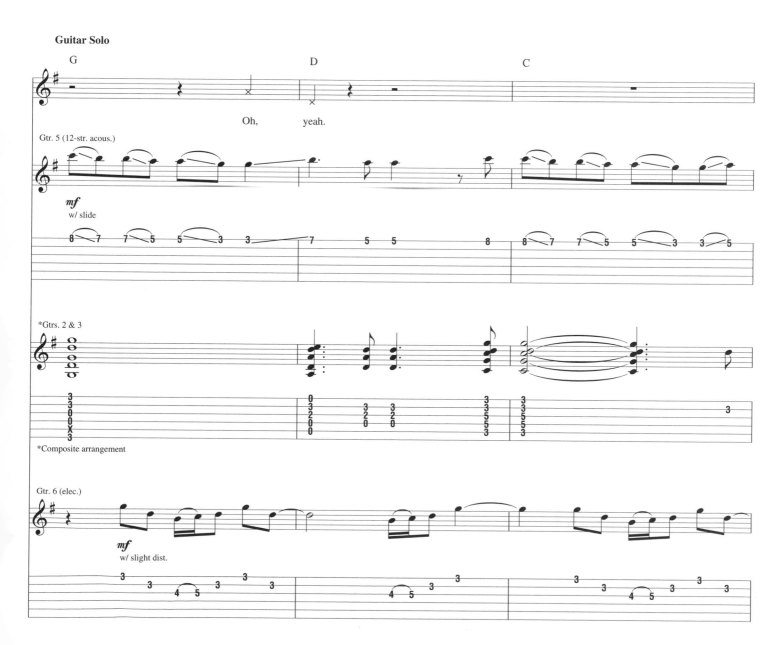

Oh, yeah.

Gtr. 5 (12-str. acous.)

mf
w/ slide

*Gtrs. 2 & 3

*Composite arrangement

Gtr. 6 (elec.)

mf
w/ slight dist.

left a reb - el with - out a clue. ___ Won't-cha

tell me what   I should   do? ___   Oh, ___

If it's just a game, ___ then we'll break down just in case. ___ Then a-

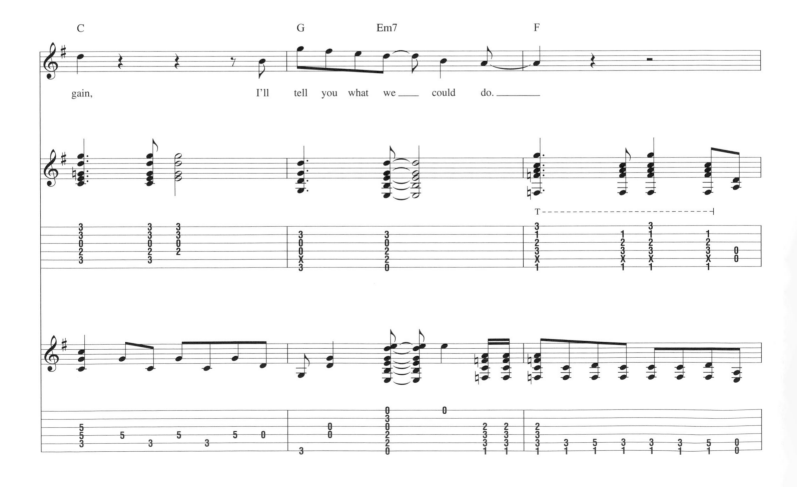

gain, I'll tell you what we ___ could do. ___

Outro

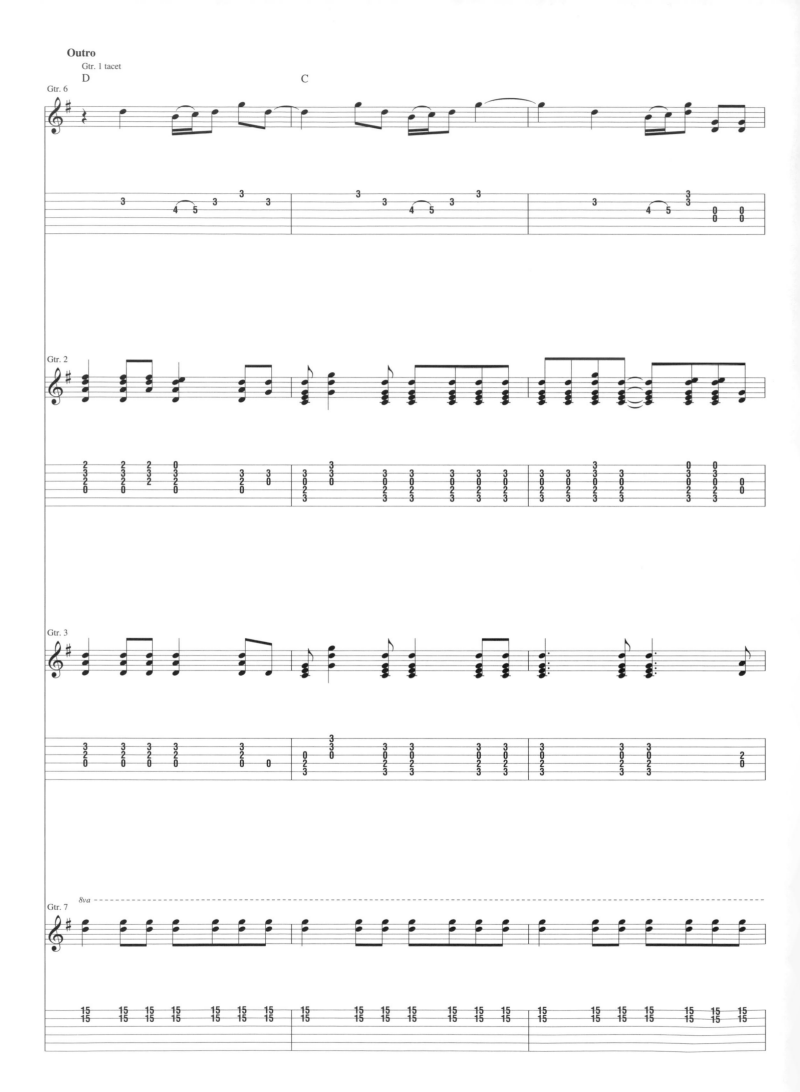

from *Sorry Ma, Forgot to Take Out the Trash*

Johnny's Gonna Die

Words and Music by Paul Westerberg

Intro

Moderately ♩ = 130

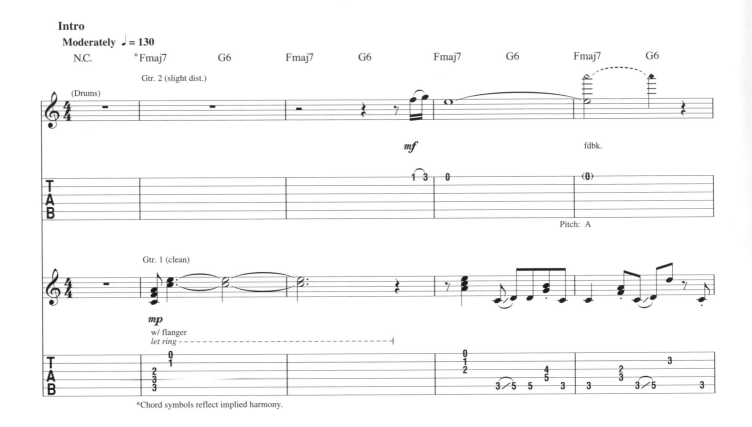

*Chord symbols reflect implied harmony.

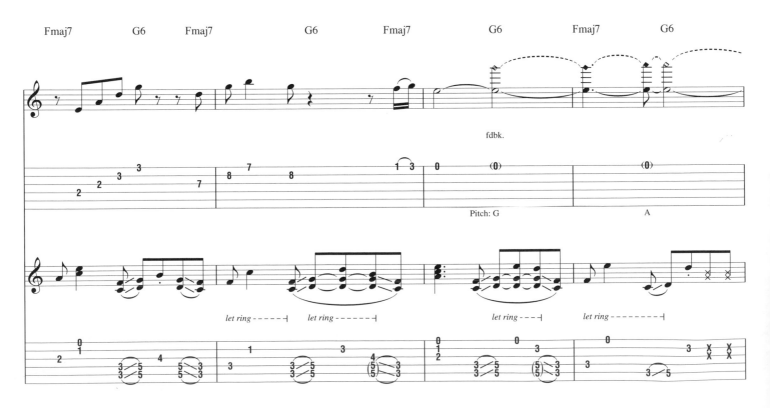

Verse

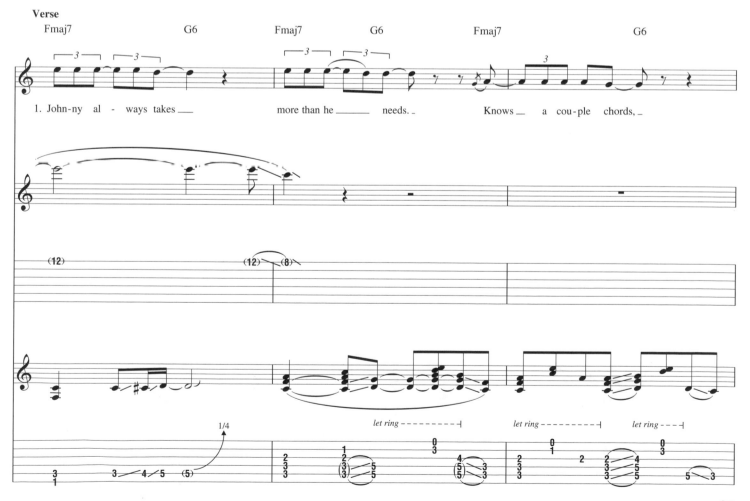

1. John-ny al - ways takes ___ more than he ___ needs. ___ Knows ___ a cou-ple chords, ___

knows a cou-ple leads. ___

Johnny al - ways needs more ___

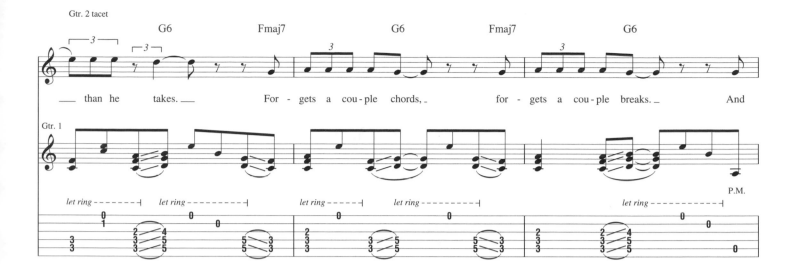

than he takes. For - gets a cou - ple chords, for - gets a cou - ple breaks. And

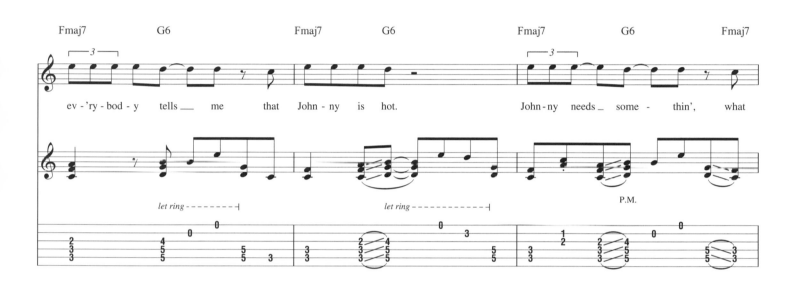

ev - 'ry - bod - y tells me that John - ny is hot. John - ny needs some - thin', what

Chorus

he ain't got. And John - ny's gon - na die.

Johnny's gonna die.   Johnny's gonna die. ___

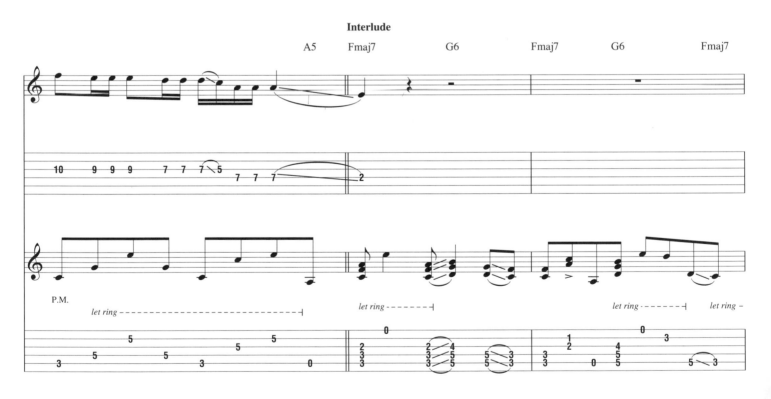

Interlude

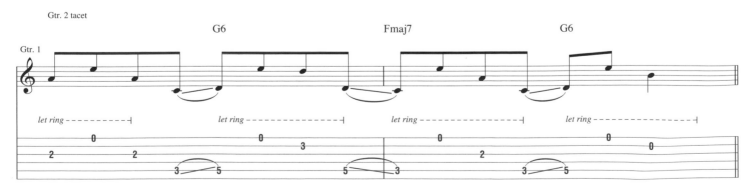

Stand - in' by the beach, and there ain't no lake. He's got

friends with - out no guts, friends what nev - er ache. In New York Cit - y, I guess it's

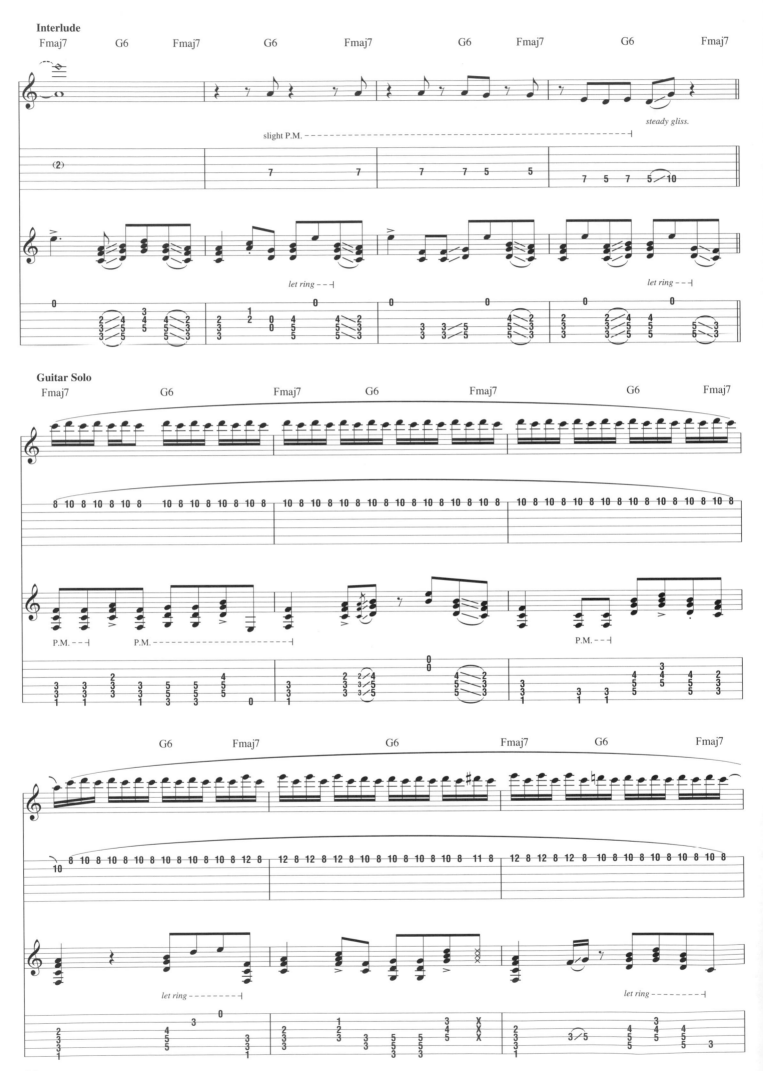

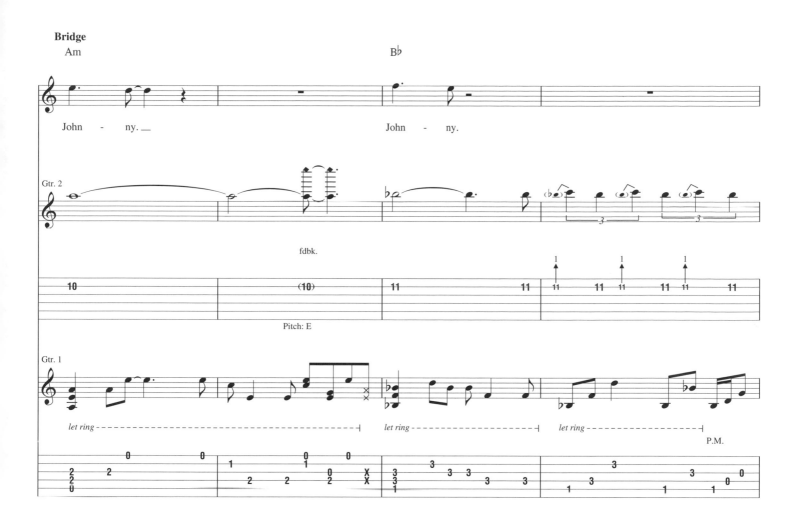

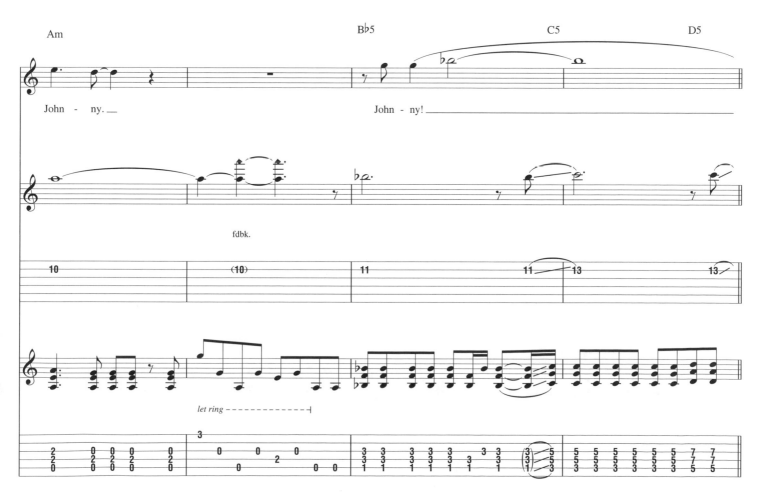

Outro

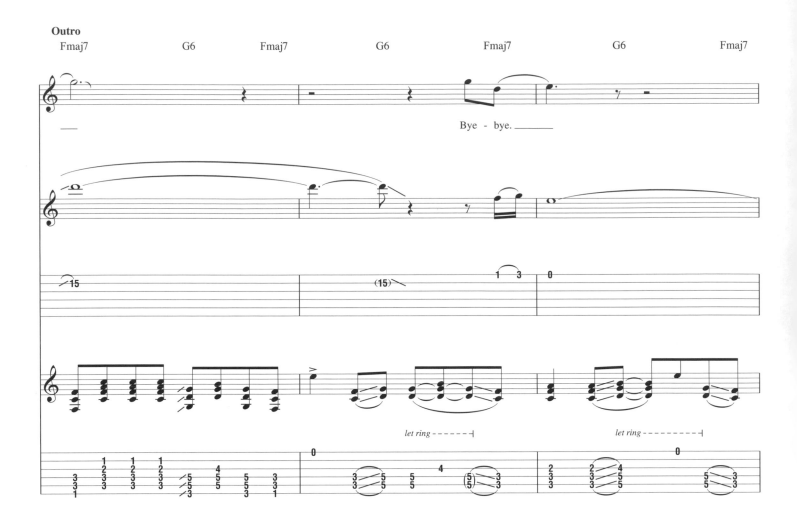

Bye - bye.

Bye - bye.   Bye - bye.

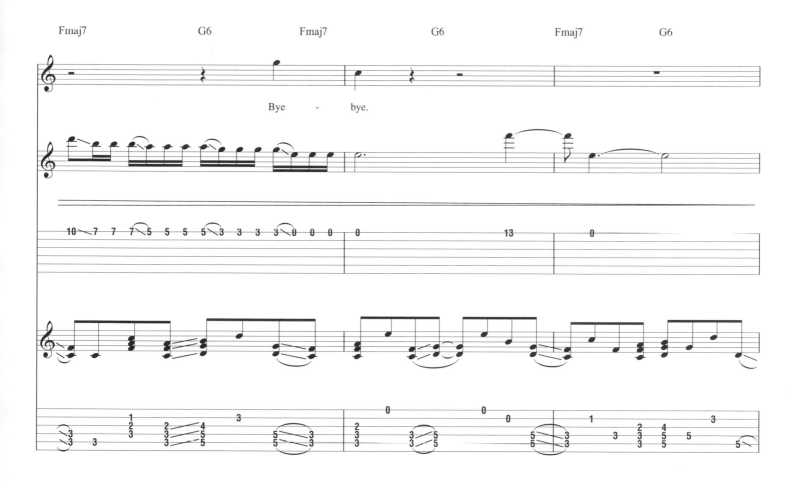

Bye - bye.

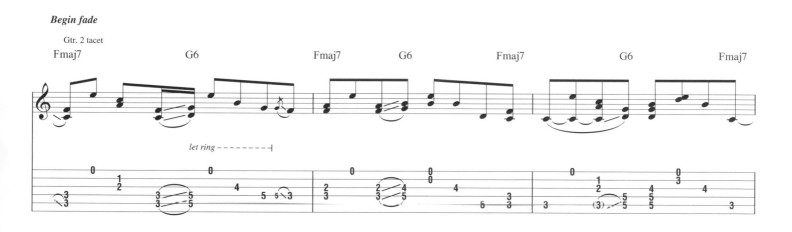

Begin fade

Gtr. 2 tacet

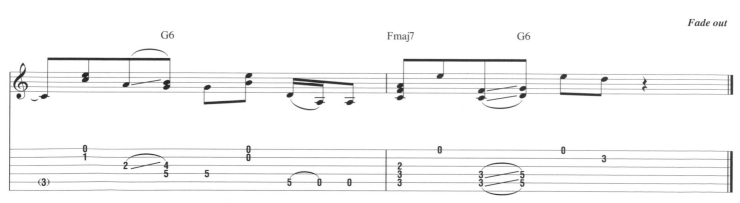

Fade out

from *Stereo*

Let the Bad Times Roll

Words and Music by Paul Westerberg

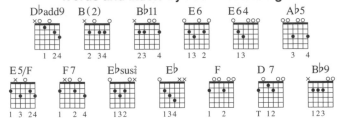

Open A tuning, down 1/2 step:
(low to high) E♭-A♭-C-E♭-A♭-C

Intro
Moderately ♩ = 85

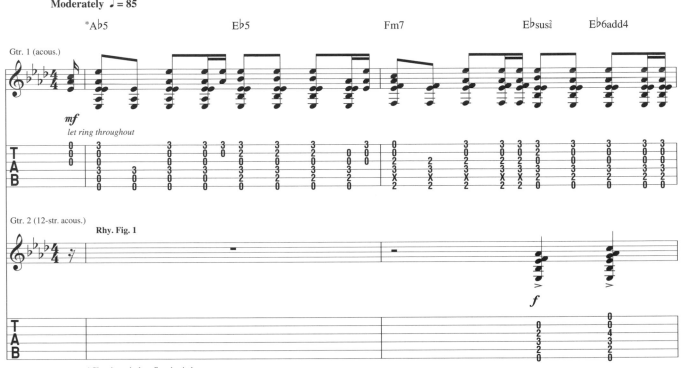

*Chord symbols reflect basic harmony.

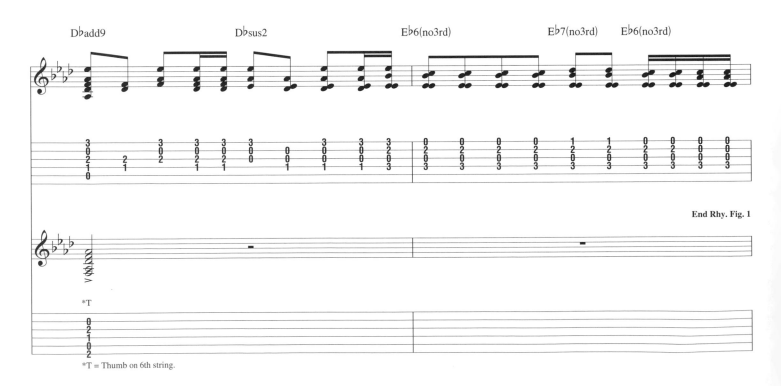

*T = Thumb on 6th string.

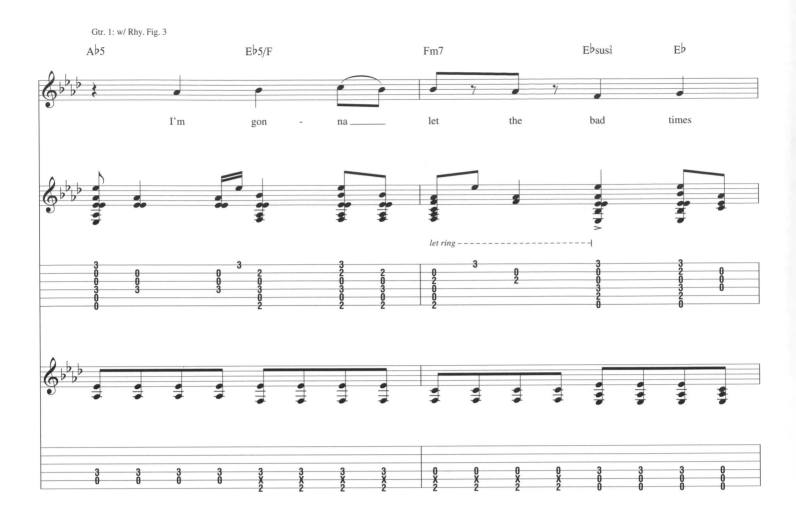

Gtr. 1: w/ Rhy. Fig. 3

A♭5   E♭5/F   Fm7   E♭sus⅔   E♭

I'm   gon -   na _____   let   the   bad   times

let ring - - - - - - - - - - - - - - - - - ⌐

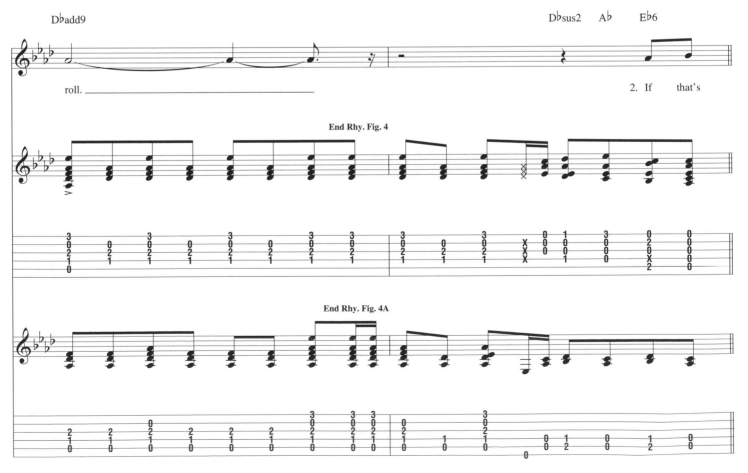

D♭add9   D♭sus2 A♭   E♭6

roll. _____   2. If   that's

End Rhy. Fig. 4

End Rhy. Fig. 4A

Gtrs. 1 & 2: w/ Rhy. Figs. 2 & 2A

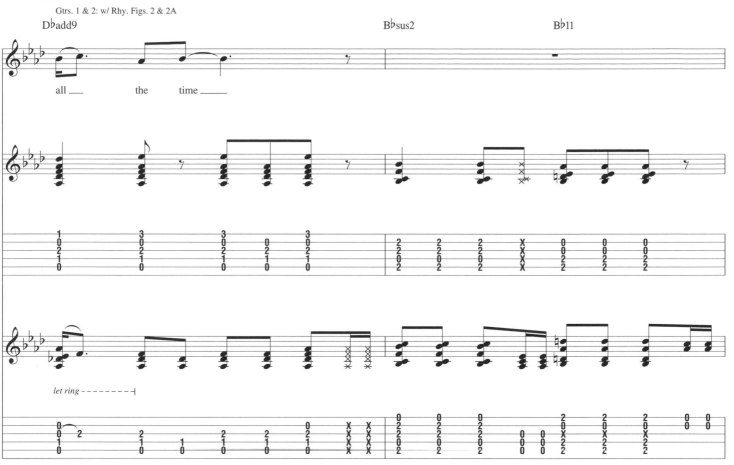

all ___ the time ___

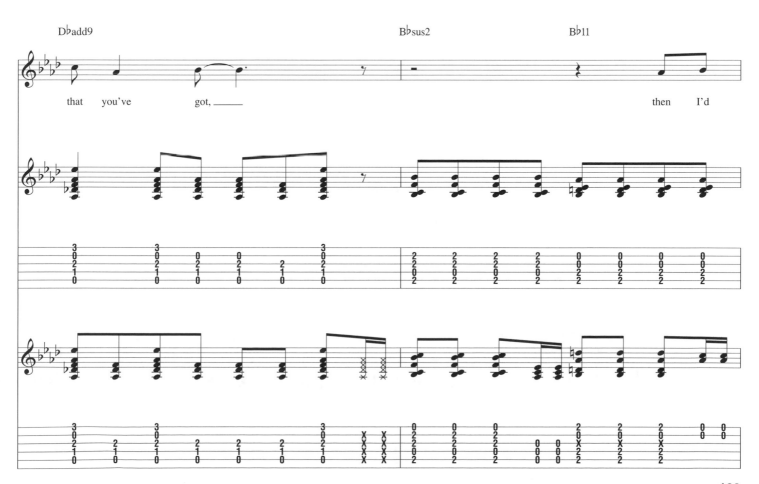

that you've got, ___ then I'd

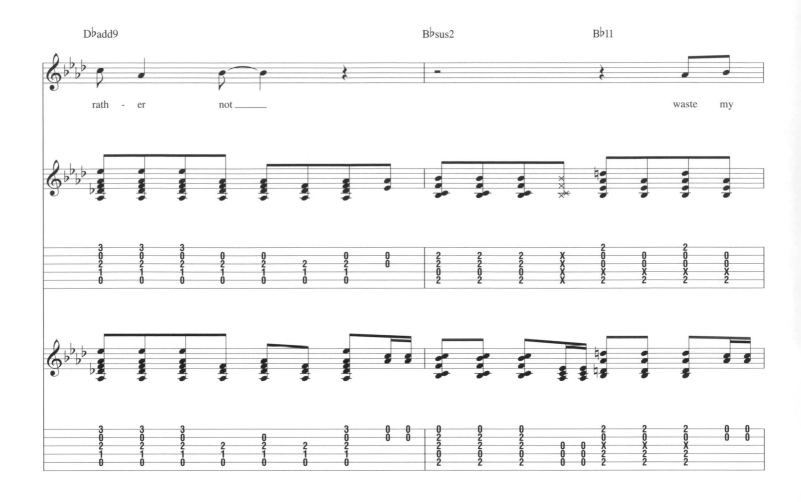

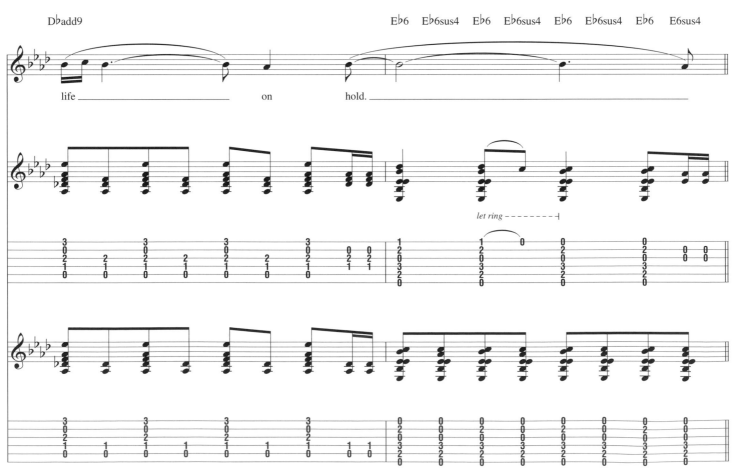

Chorus

Gtr. 1: w/ Rhy. Fig. 3 (1 3/4 times)
Gtr. 2: w/ Rhy. Fig. 1 (2 times)
Gtrs. 3 & 4: w/ Rhy. Figs. 4 & 4A

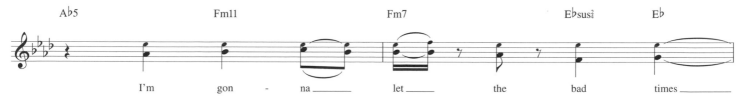

I'm   gon - na _____   let _____   the   bad   times _____

_____ roll.   I'm   gon - na _____

let _____   the   bad   times   roll.

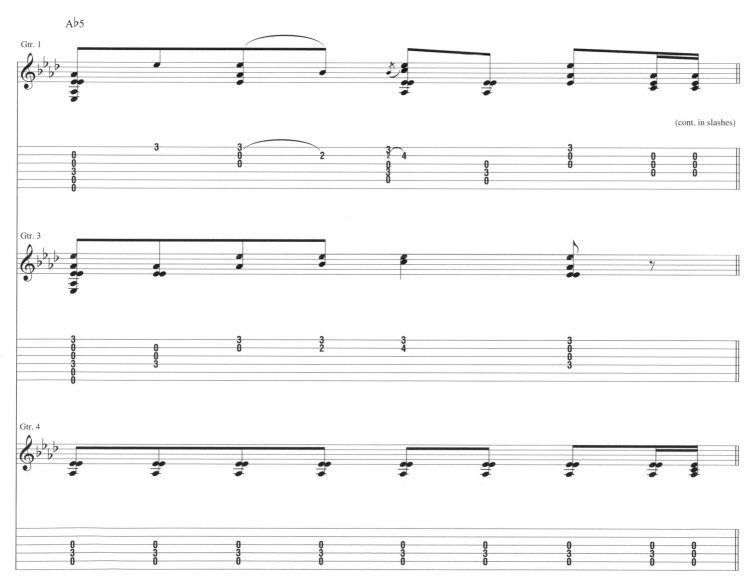

(cont. in slashes)

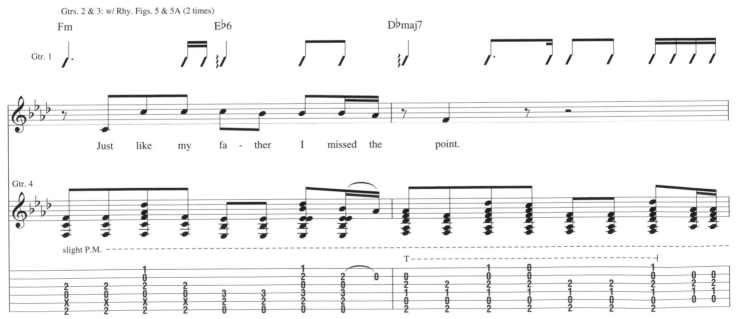

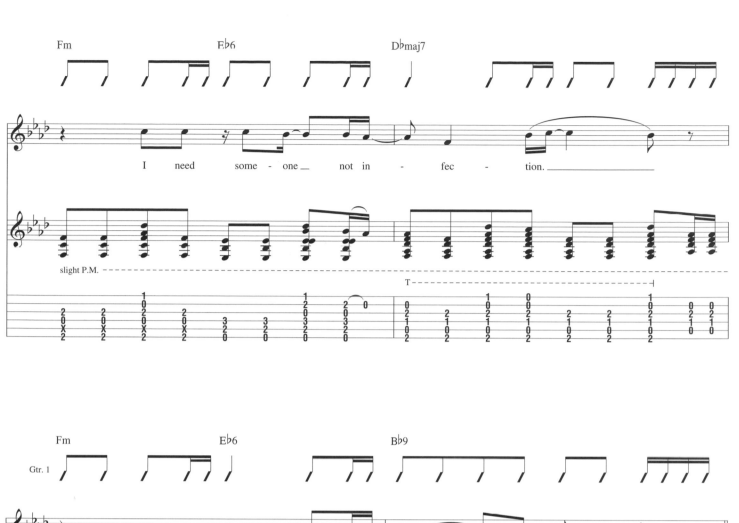

I need some - one ___ not in - fec - tion. ___

Just add wa - ter I'm dis - ap - point - ed. ___

Verse

Gtr. 1: w/ Rhy. Fig. 2
Gtrs. 3 & 4: w/ Rhy. Fig. 6A (3 times)

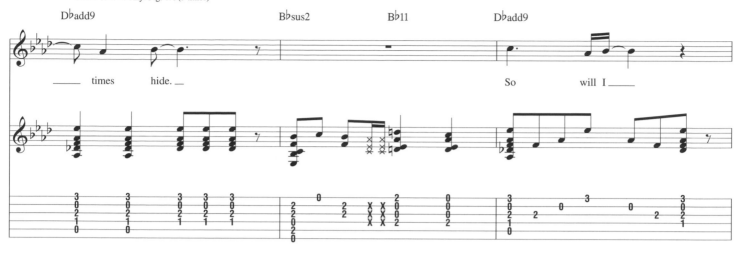

_____ times   hide. _____   So   will   I _____

watch the world _____   roll _____ by _____

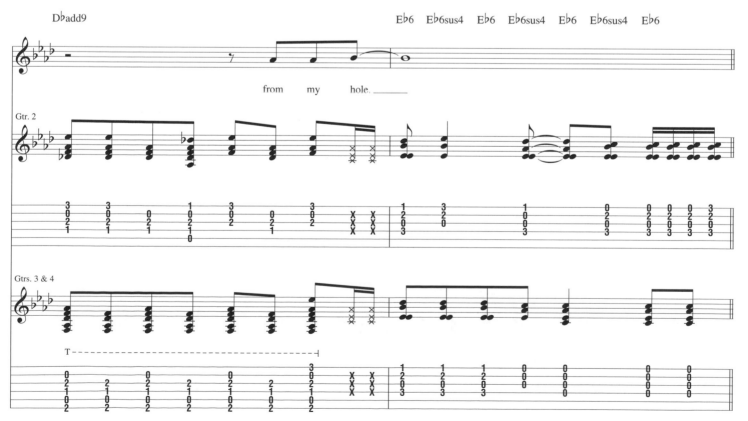

from   my   hole. _____

Outro

Play 4 times and fade

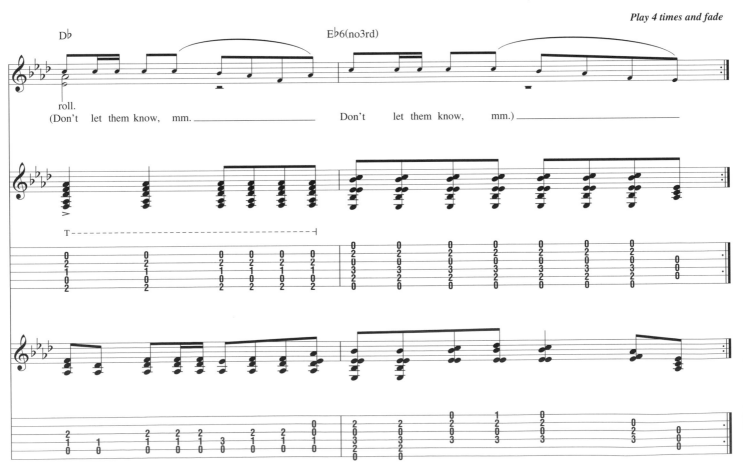

from *All Shook Down*

Merry Go Round

Words and Music by Paul Westerberg

Verse

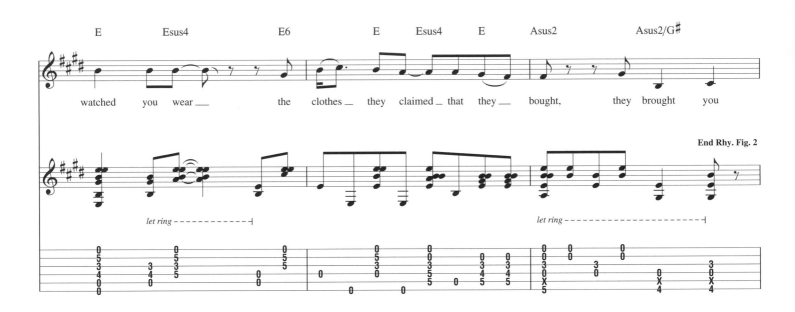

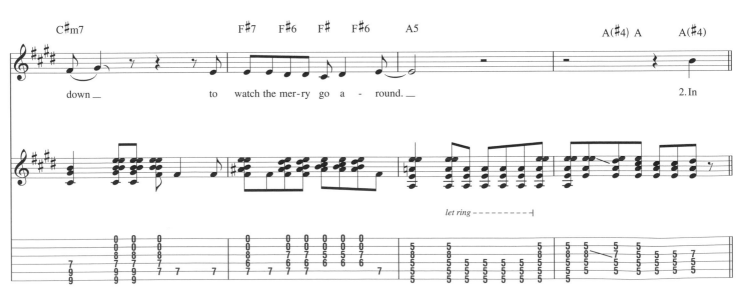

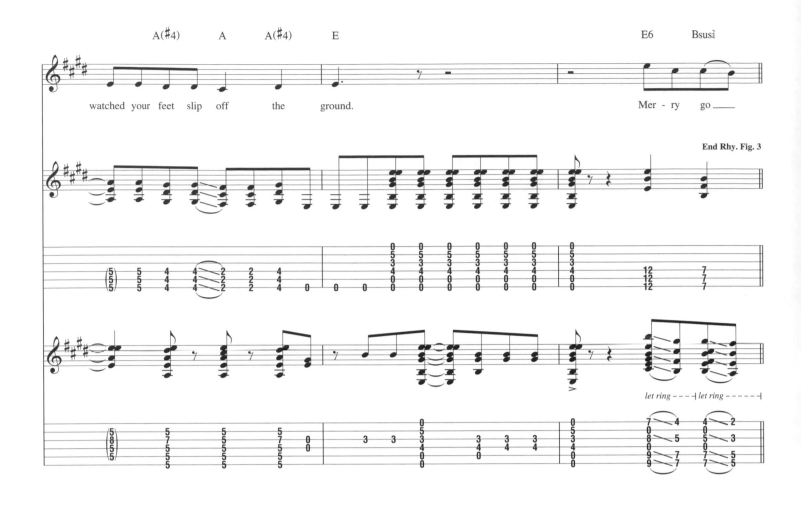

Chorus

Chorus

Gtrs. 1 & 2: w/ Rhy. Fig. 4 (1st 6 meas.)
Gtr. 3: w/ Rhy. Fig. 4A (1st 6 meas.)
Gtr. 4 tacet

123

Bridge

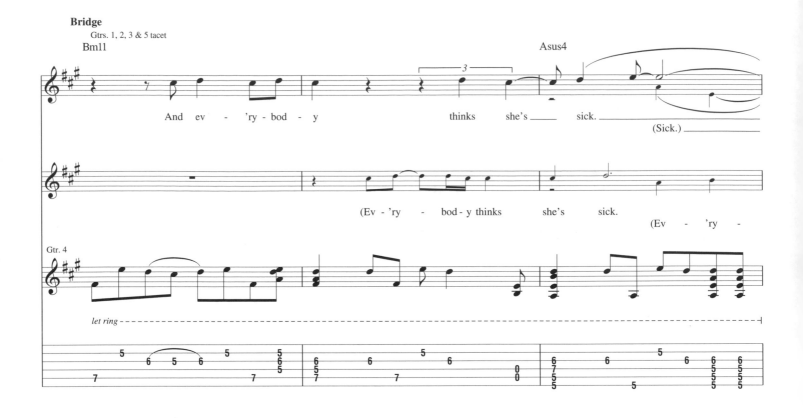

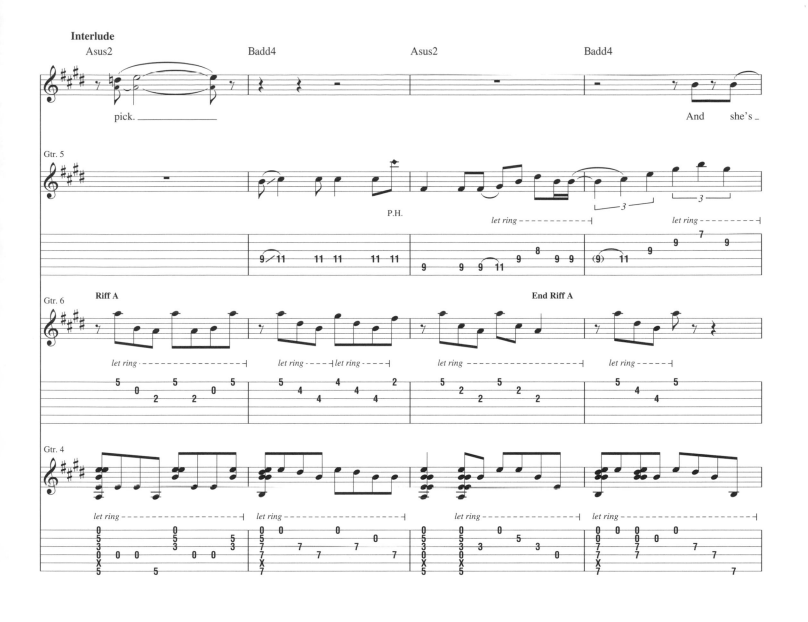

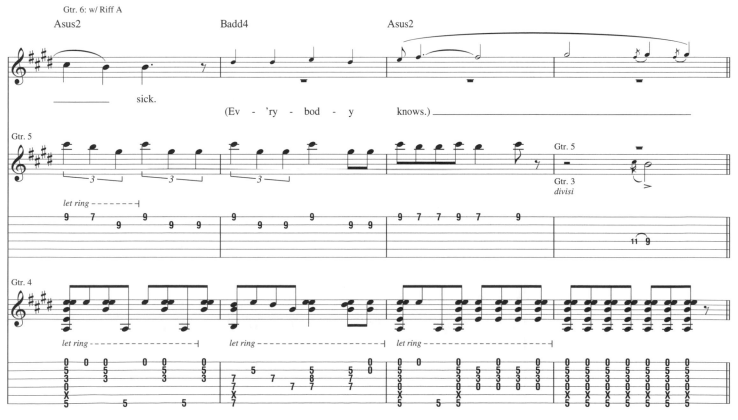

Guitar Solo

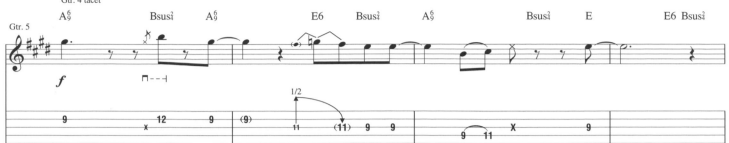

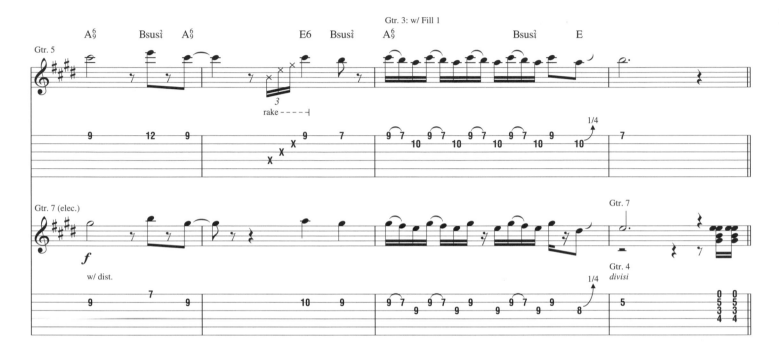

Verse

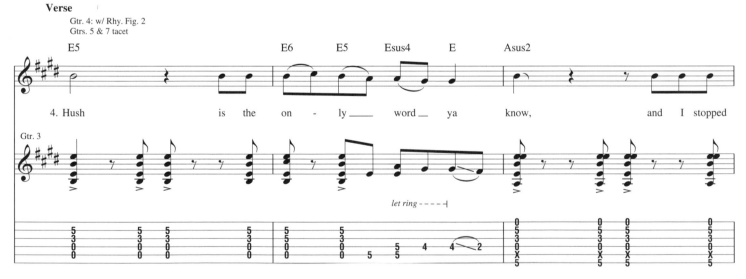

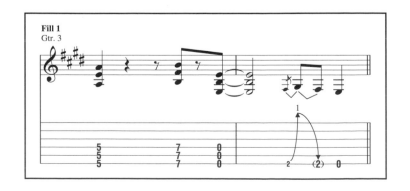

Chorus

Gtrs. 1 & 2: w/Rhy. Fig. 4 (1st 6 meas.)
Gtr. 3: w/ Rhy. Fig. 4A
Gtr. 4 tacet

And when she sleeps, she's free. ___ Mer - ry go ___

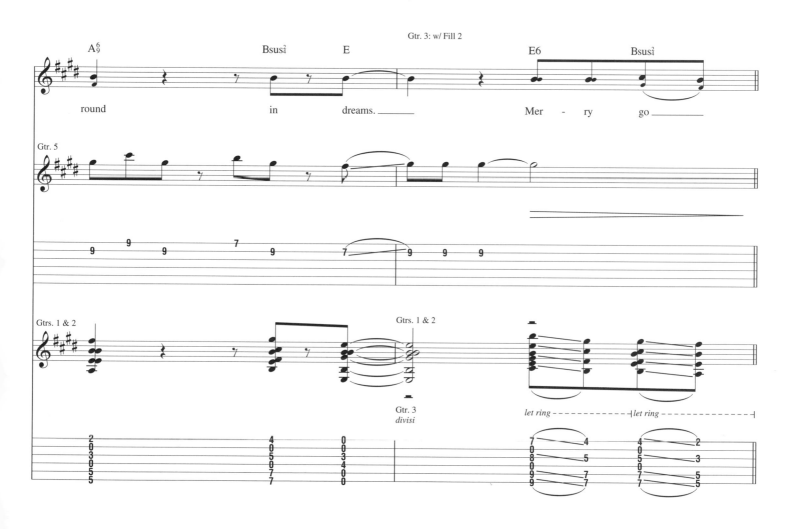

round in dreams. ___ Mer - ry go ___

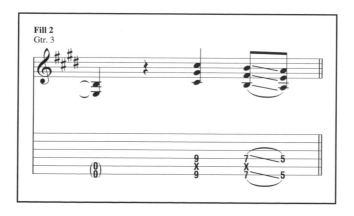

Outro

Gtr. 3: w/ Rhy. Fig. 1 (till fade)

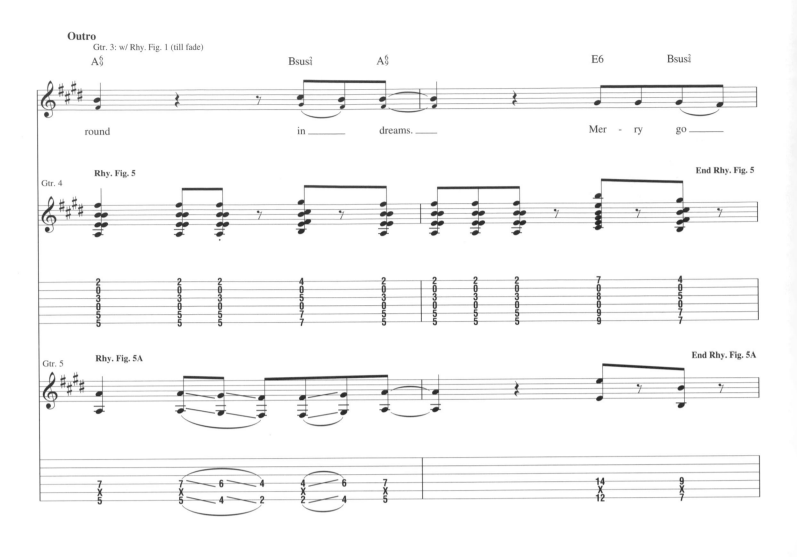

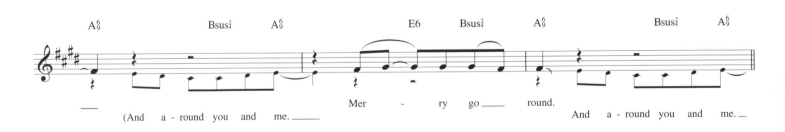

Play 3 times and fade

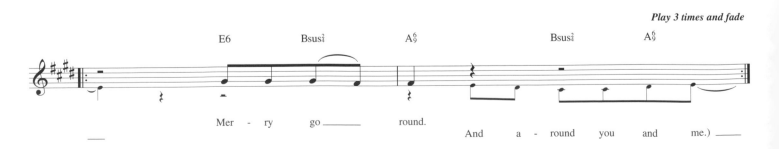

130

from *Sorry Ma, Forgot to Take Out the Trash*

Shiftless When Idle

Words and Music by Paul Westerberg

Tune down 1/2 step:
(low to high) Eb-Ab-Db-Gb-Bb-Eb

*Chord symbols reflect overall harmony.

Pitch: F♮

**Harmonic located three-fourths
the distance between 2nd & 3rd fret.

Chorus

I ain't got no i - dols. I ain't got _ much taste. _ I'm

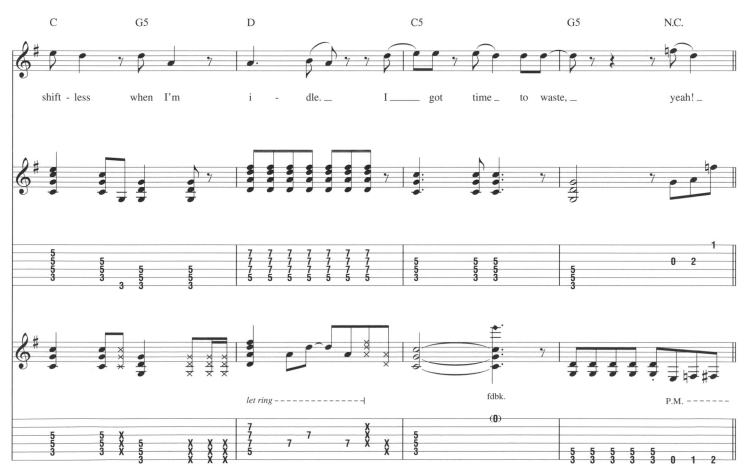

shift - less when I'm i - dle. _ I _ got time _ to waste, _ yeah! _

Interlude

G5

2. They

Verse

G5　　　　　　　　　　　　　　　　　　　　　E　　Esus4 E　　　Esus4 E

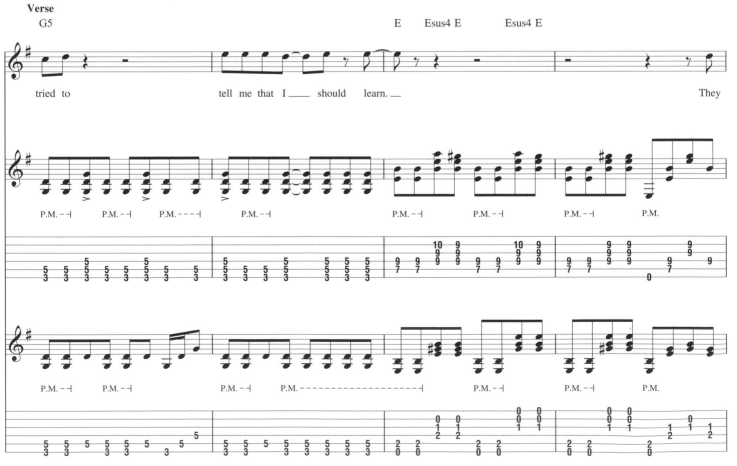

tried to　　　　　　tell me that I ___ should　learn. ___　　　　　　　They

134

told me   it's best I   wait   my   turn,   yeah.   And

Chorus

I can't   wait   for - ev - er.   I can't   wait   that   long.   I'm

shift - less when I'm i - dle. ___ I wan - na play ___ this... _____

Interlude

G5

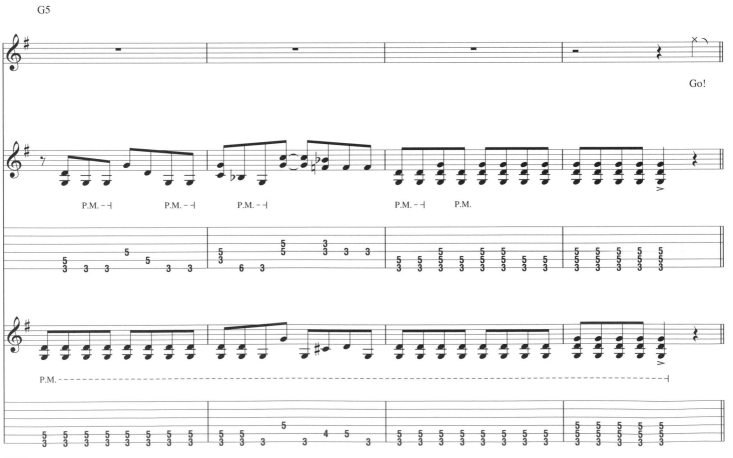

Go!

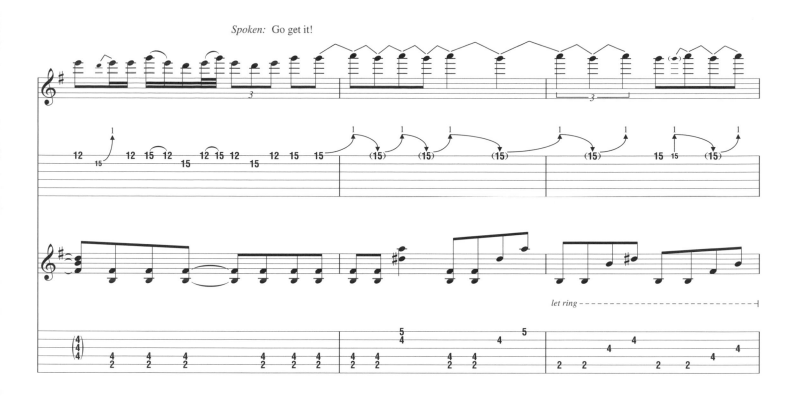

Spoken: Go get it!

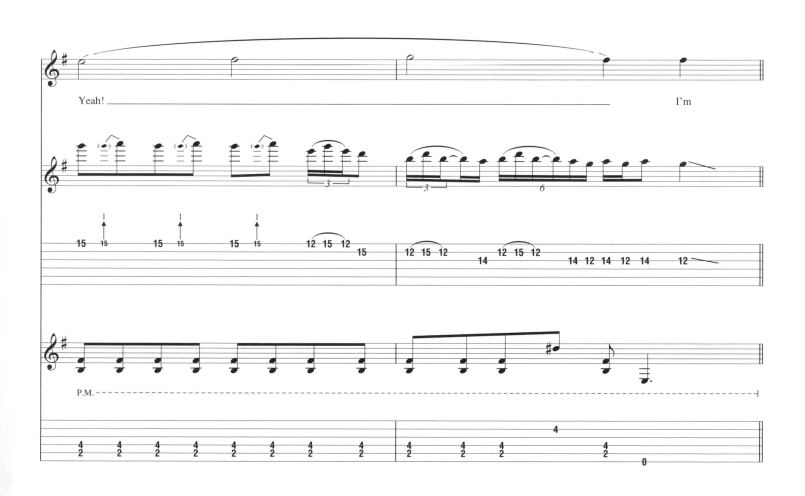

Yeah! _____ I'm

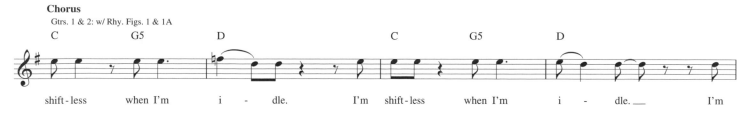

Chorus
Gtrs. 1 & 2: w/ Rhy. Figs. 1 & 1A

C   G5   D   C   G5   D

shift-less   when I'm   i - dle.   I'm shift-less   when I'm   i - dle. ___   I'm

from *Pleased to Meet Me*

Skyway

Words and Music by Paul Westerberg

Capo III

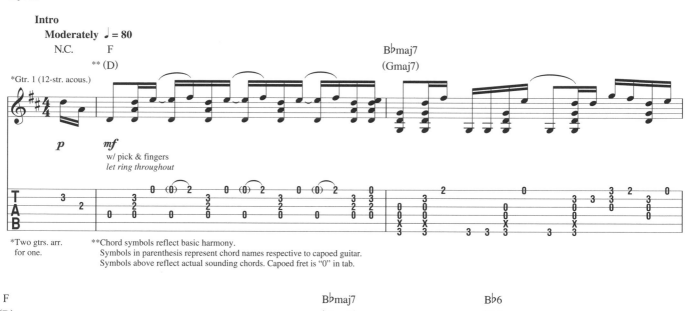

*Two gtrs. arr. for one.
**Chord symbols reflect basic harmony.
Symbols in parenthesis represent chord names respective to capoed guitar.
Symbols above reflect actual sounding chords. Capoed fret is "0" in tab.

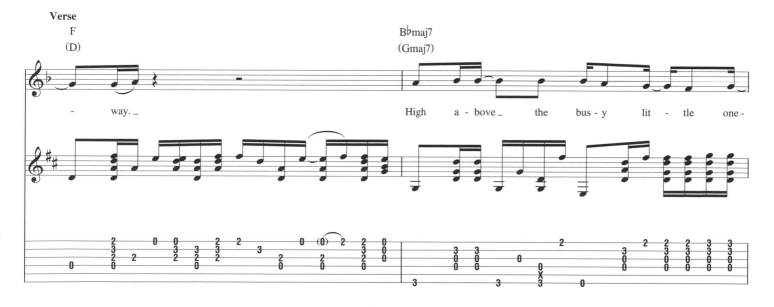

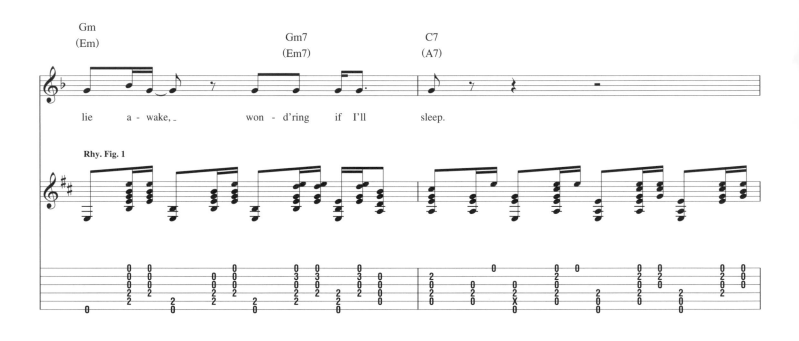

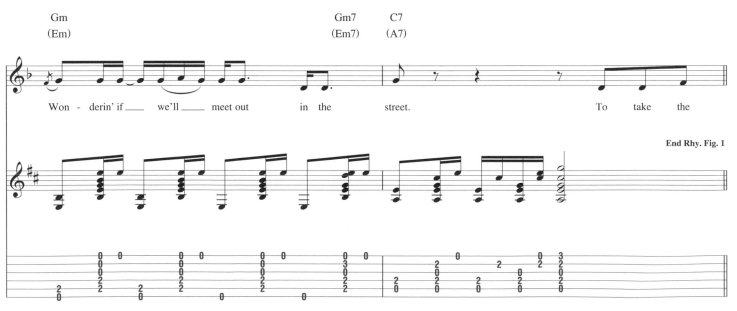

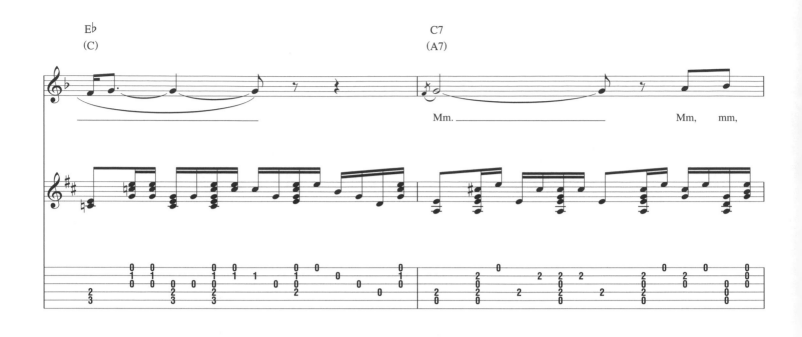

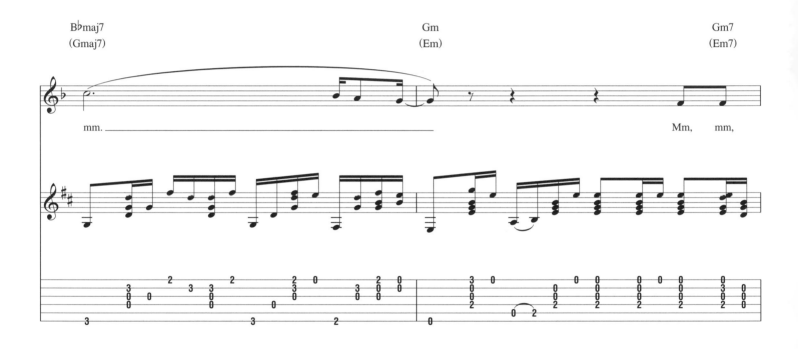

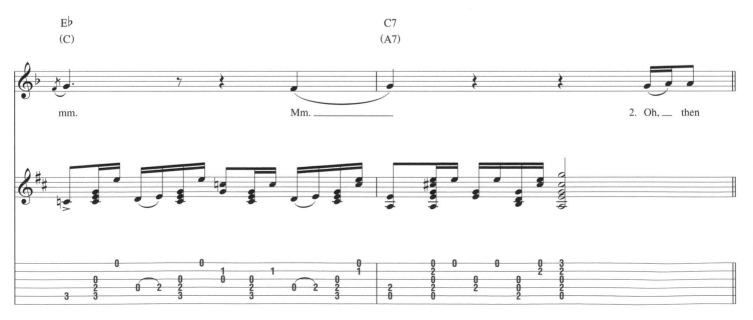

Verse

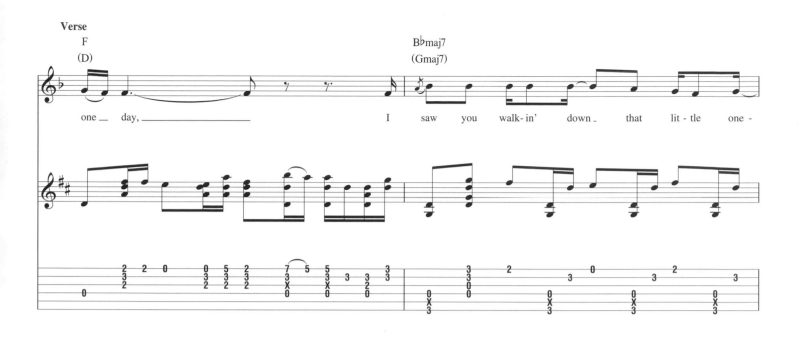

one __ day, _____ I saw you walk-in' down __ that lit - tle one -

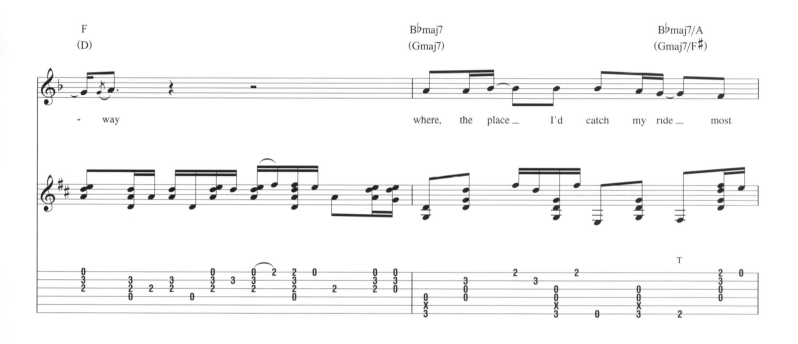

- way where, the place __ I'd catch my ride __ most

ev - 'ry day. __ There was - n't a damn __ thing I could do __ or __ say, __

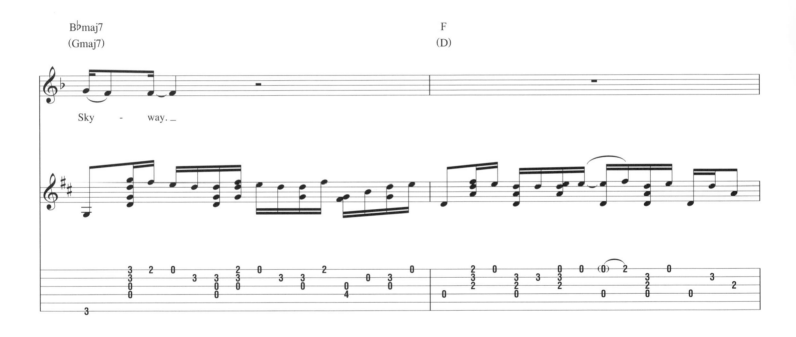

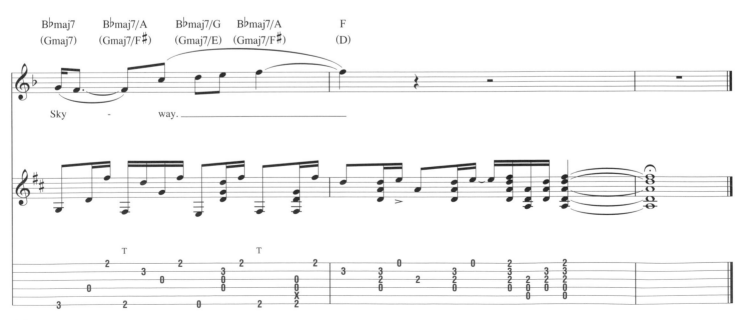

from *Let It Be*

Unsatisfied

Words and Music by Paul Westerberg

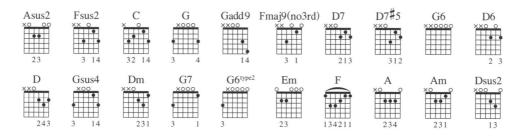

Intro
Moderately ♩ = 119

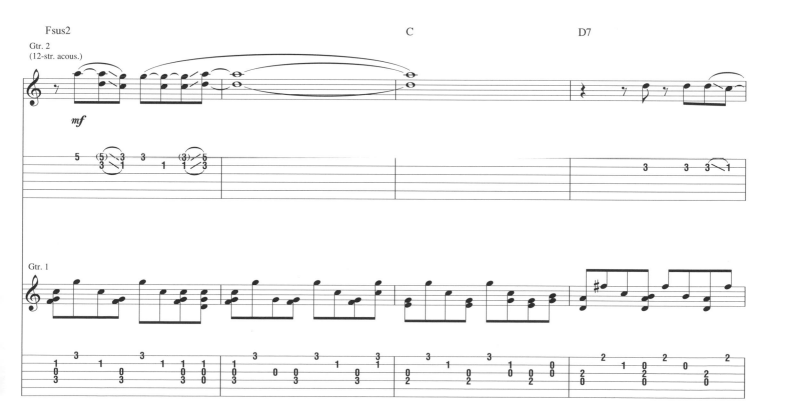

*Doubled throughout w/ 12-str. acous.
**Chord symbols reflect implied harmony.

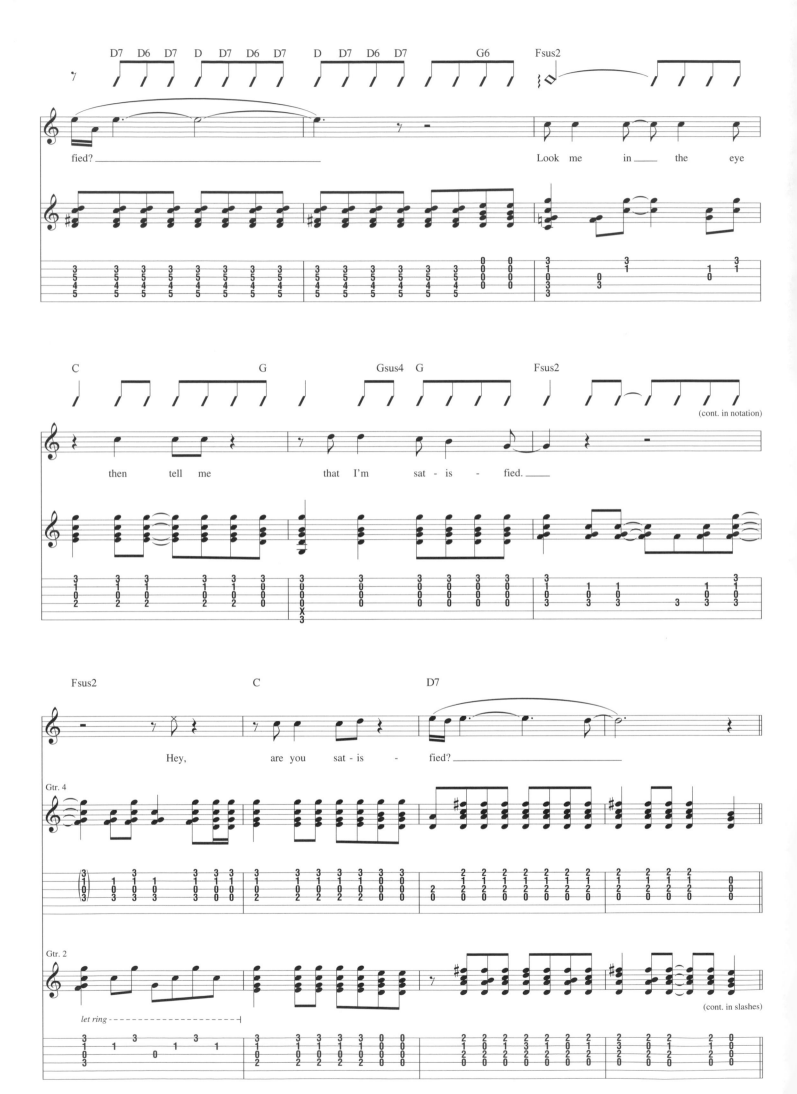

Verse

Gtr. 2

Dm   G7   G6^{type2}   Dm   G7   G6^{type2}

1. And it goes _____ so slow - ly on. ____

Gtr. 5 (elec.)

p < *mf*
w/ clean tone

*Vol. swell throughout.

Gtr. 4

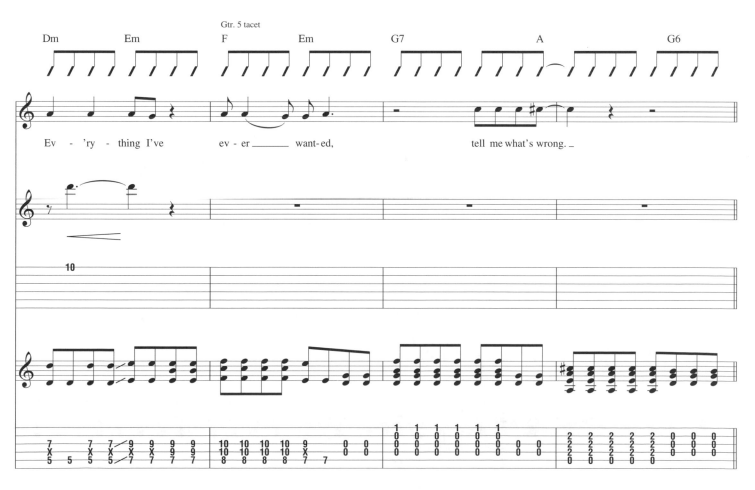

Gtr. 5 tacet

Dm   Em   F   Em   G7   A   G6^{type2}

Ev - 'ry - thing I've ev - er ____ want- ed, tell me what's wrong. ___

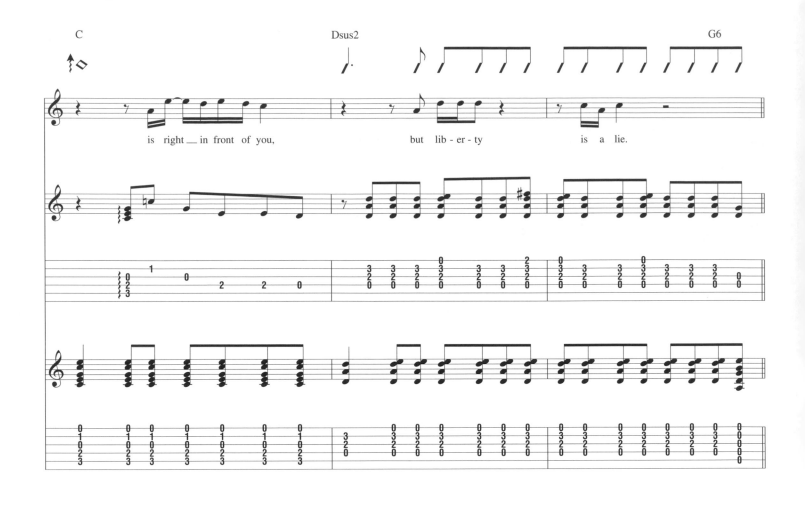

is right __ in front of you,   but lib - er - ty   is a lie.

Chorus

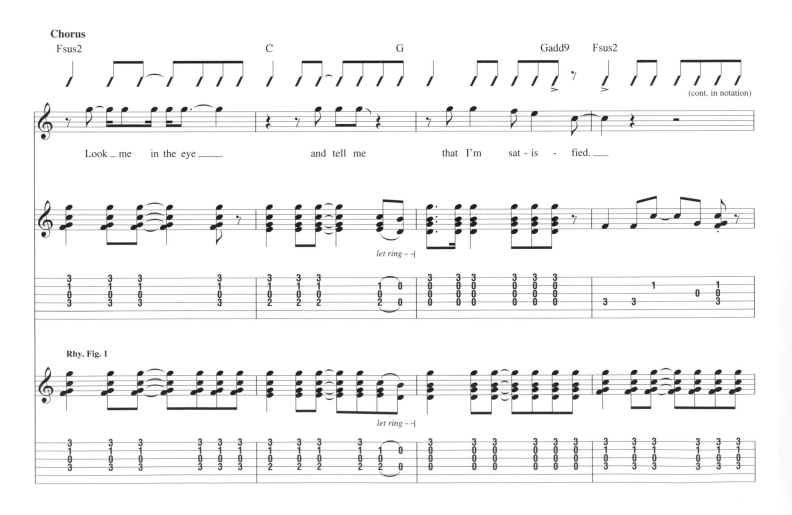

Look __ me in the eye ____   and tell me   that I'm sat - is - fied. ____

(cont. in notation)

let ring -

Rhy. Fig. 1

let ring -

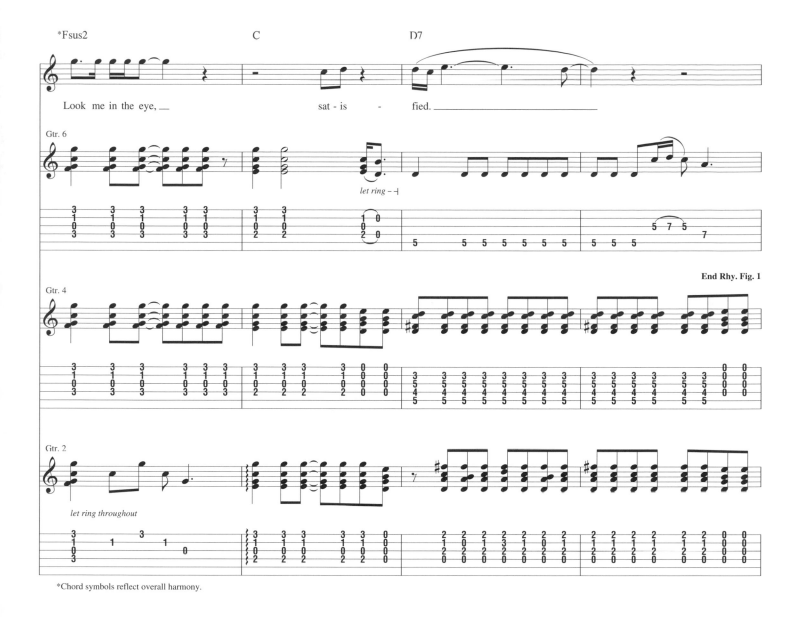

Look me in the eye, ___ sat - is - fied.

*Chord symbols reflect overall harmony.

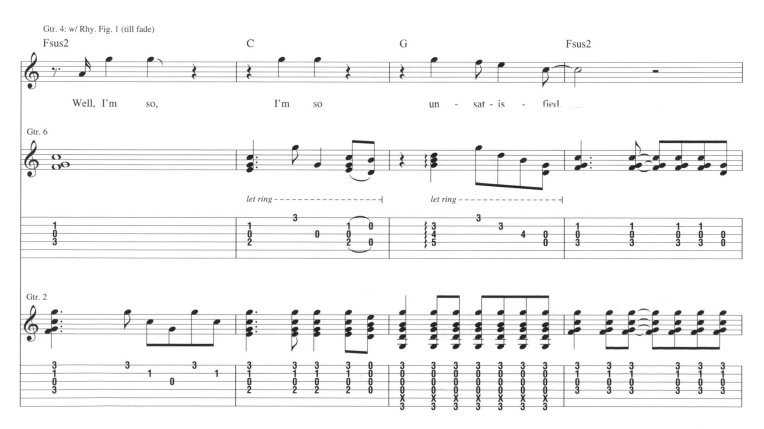

Well, I'm so, I'm so un - sat - is - fied.

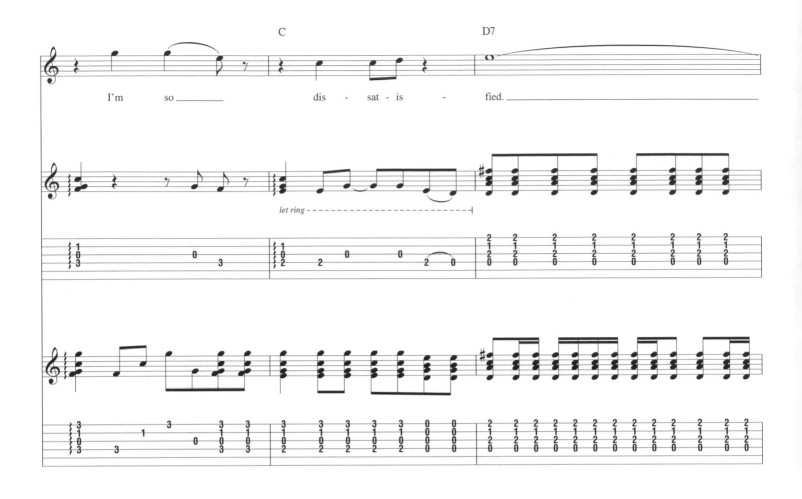

I'm so _____ dis - sat - is - fied. _____

let ring - |

I'm so,   I'm so

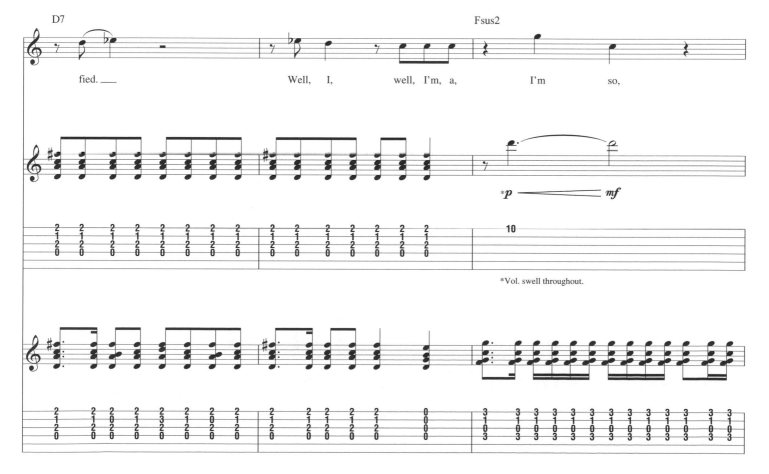

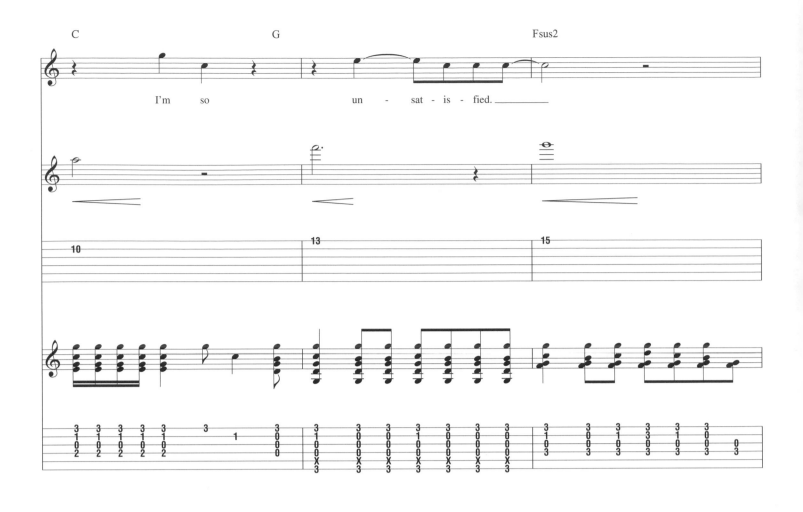

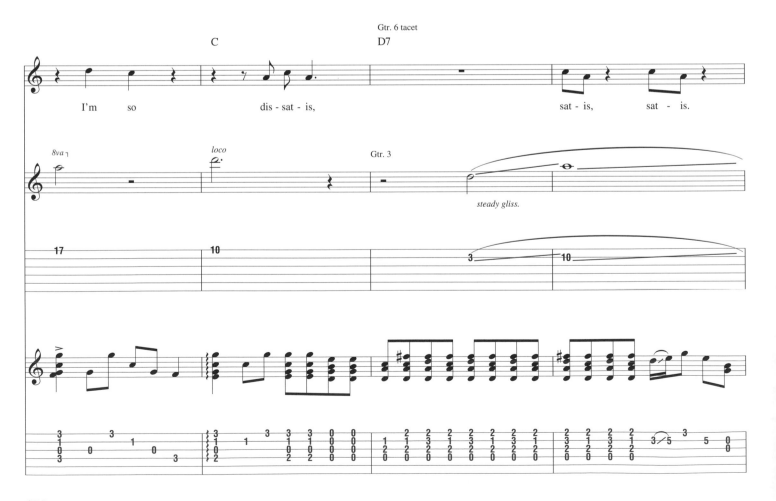

Begin fade

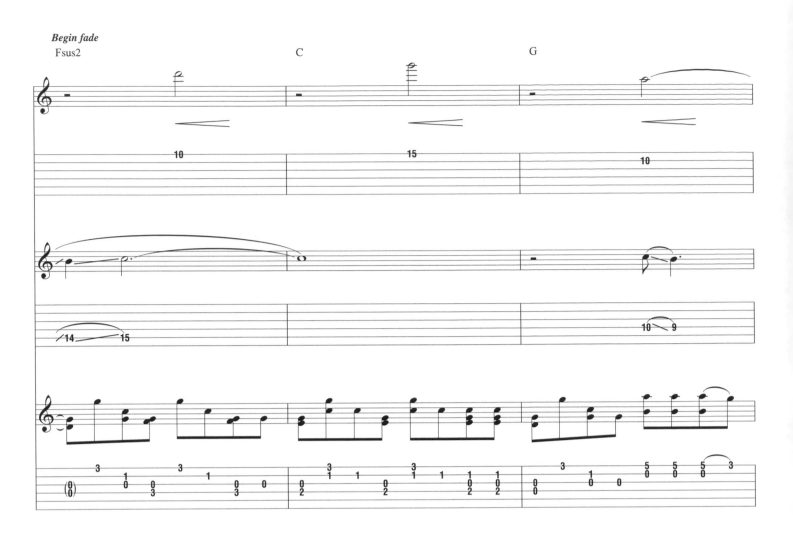

Fade out